FOLK ART Christmas Ornaments

FOLK ART Christmas Ornaments

How to Make Them

MAXINE KENNY

ARCO PUBLISHING, INC.
NEW YORK

Published by Arco Publishing, Inc.
215 Park Avenue South, New York, N.Y. 10003

Library of Congress Cataloging in Publication Data

Kenny, Maxine.
  Folk art Christmas ornaments.

  Bibliography: p.
  1. Christmas decorations. 2. Folk art.
I. Title.
TT900.C4K46 1985   745.594'1   85-7431
ISBN 0-668-06376-9 (cloth edition)

Printed in the United States of America

10 9 8 7 6 5 4 3 2 1

For Don, my husband,
who helped make this book

Contents

Foreword

This book attempts to acquaint readers with the traditional folk arts of many countries—including our own—and to enhance our celebration of Christmas by showing how to make Christmas ornaments using folk art techniques. The ornaments are organized by decorating theme and span several centuries of tree-trimming, from the Paradise Tree of medieval times to a modern-day Country Christmas Tree. Whenever possible, I have retold Christmas legends and given historical background along with the ornament instructions and pattern pieces. Some of the ornaments are imitations of things made for everyday use, such as the "tin" quilt templates; others are folk objects that are used for special holidays and festivals, such as the Chinese dragon, the Ukrainian Easter eggs, and the Danish Jul Nisse (or Christmas Elf). The amazing variety of the folk art ornaments will perhaps inspire you to be creative and experiment with other tree trims using the techniques explained here. You will discover that folk arts from different countries can blend quite effectively.

I have indicated in the text whenever the ornaments are *adaptations* of the traditional folk objects. I have also adapted the ornaments if authentic materials are not available, if special skills are needed to complete an object, or if I have wanted to make an ornament more contemporary.

Photographs, line drawings, and step-by-step directions serve as guides for constructing the ornaments, some of which are simple and quick to make and some of which are more complex and take more time and patience. You do not have to strive for perfection when making the ornaments—traditional folk art is the humble and unsophisticated handiwork of untrained, ordinary people. Perspective, proportion, and technique are not absolutely necessary. Little imperfections often add a special charm.

Learning about and crafting folk objects from different countries can help us understand and appreciate cultural likenesses and differences as we become acquainted first-hand with the exciting customs of other lands.

I'm sure you'll find pleasure in the individual and naive artistic expression so evident in folk art. You'll also discover that your most beautiful and cherished ornaments for Christmas are those you've made yourself.

MAXINE KENNY

Introduction

The Christmas tree was introduced to America by German immigrants in the eighteenth century. Christmas itself, however, was little celebrated in Colonial America, except in the Anglican and Catholic Colonies of the South and where the Germans, Dutch, and Moravians settled. The Puritans, who settled New England, forbade any observance of Christmas celebrations, since they believed no day should be more important than the Sabbath. After the American Revolution, Christmas trees started to appear throughout America. These early trees were unpretentious: They were only a few feet high, set on tables, and decorated with modest and simple ornaments such as nuts, homemade cookies, strings of popcorn, and apples.

Tree-trimming was not widely practiced in America until the Victorian period. By the middle of the nineteenth century, people living in the cities could buy special toys and imported glass ornaments for their trees. Nonetheless, most people, because of their rural isolation or a shortage of cash, continued to make their ornaments from spare materials and from materials that nature provided.

Around the turn of the twentieth century, the Christmas tree became very popular in America, and larger, floor-to-ceiling trees replaced table trees. These trees were often decorated with both store-bought and homemade ornaments. People who did not have a tree at home could enjoy the community tree set up in the local schoolhouse, town hall, or church. By 1930 the decorated Christmas tree had become a significant part of the American Christmas.

The essence of every culture is reflected and expressed by the common people through their folklore and their folk art, handed down from generation to generation. America, the melting pot of nations, has been enriched by the integration of these folk traditions into our own culture. Modern America owes much of its enjoyment of the celebration of Christmas to the customs, beliefs, traditions, and folk arts contributed by immigrants to its shores.

Supplies

The folk artist of today is more fortunate than the folk artist of the past in that the materials needed can be purchased from fabric stores, craft and hobby shops, garden centers, and florist shops. However, much of the joy of making folk art objects comes from recycling discards from home and using materials that nature provides free of charge. Search your yard, nearby parks, woods, and fields for cones, pods, grasses, vines, dried flowers, and nuts. Look for fabric and yarn scraps in your sewing basket, for wood scraps in the garage; and don't throw away the eggshells from your kitchen. These are just a few of the materials that can be incorporated imaginatively into folk art Christmas ornaments.

In addition to your "found" materials, you'll need other supplies that you may have to purchase in order to make the Christmas folk ornaments contained in this book.

Acrylic Paint—water-based paint that can be thinned with water but dries waterproof; sold in tubes or jars. Acrylic polymer medium is a sort of glaze mixed with acrylic colors to create a more adhesive water-resistant gloss finish.

Activa® Products, Inc. Celluclay—a non-toxic instant papier mâché that can be molded like clay and mixes with water

Chenille Stems—"stems" 12 inches long, similar to pipe cleaners; they come in a variety of colors

Corn Husks—commercially prepared natural husks can be found in hobby and craft shops and also some grocery stores, which stock them for tamales

Elmer's® Glue-All—a white, all-purpose, quick-setting, clear-drying glue

Excelsior—thin wood shavings used to line and cushion gift fruit baskets; available at craft shops and florist shops.

Floral Stemming Tape—tape that conceals wires and is used for attaching stems together

Florist's Tying Wire—22 gauge wire, uncovered

Gesso—a pre-mixed plasterlike material that creates a waterproof undercoating and prepares surfaces for painting in all media

Glass Stains—permanent, transparent colors, non-toxic and water reducible

Gold Leaf Enamel—fast-drying, high gloss paint, available in model and hobby shops, paint stores, and hardware stores

Krylon Spray Fixative®—permanent protective coating for all finished art work that dries in minutes and comes in crystal clear or matte finish

Metallic Craft Trims—spangles, glitter trims, sequins

Metylan Art Paste—a paste for papier mâché, non-toxic, odorless and colorless, that won't "sour," lump, or stain. If this is not available to you, try one of the following substitutes: equal parts of white glue and water mixed; wheat paste mixed with water; or paste made with flour and water.

Nylon Fishing Line—thin, clear, strong line with which to hang ornaments

Origami Paper—special paper for folding that can be found in art supply stores

Plaster of Paris—a powder to mix with water to form a quick-setting paste

Plastic-Foam Balls—balls to be used as a base that can be found in hobby and craft shops

Polyester Fiberfill—filling for stuffing ornaments that can be found in fabric stores

Raffia—rush-like material for weaving and wrapping, usually carried in hobby and craft shops

Reeds—$\frac{1}{16}$-inch diameter reeds, the most popular size for basket-weaving, can be found in hobby and craft shops

Stitch Witchery®—a two-sided, iron-on bonding mesh stocked by fabric stores and sewing departments

Vogart® Ball Point Paint—fabric paint in tubes, used to decorate and "embroider" fabric, that is quick-drying and comes in a variety of colors

Weldwood® Wood Filler—a filler to repair wood that can be found in hardware, paint, or lumber stores.

Westwood® Ovencraft Clay—ready-to-use molding clay, non-toxic and non-staining, that can be painted with acrylic, enamel, tempera, or watercolors and hardens after baking in the oven of your kitchen stove for one hour at 350°. It makes lasting, durable objects.

Wooden Beads

How to Enlarge Patterns

Most of the patterns in this book will need to be enlarged. To enlarge a pattern, you must transfer the pattern from its smaller grid to a larger grid. To make a larger grid, mark off squares in the size indicated for a full size pattern; however, keep the same number of squares that are on the smaller grid. Then, copy the outline of the pattern from the small grid to your grid of larger squares, drawing in the lines one square at a time. When you finish, connect the lines smoothly, and you'll have an actual-size pattern ready to cut out.

Tree Themes

Frontier Tree

Christmas on the American frontier was often a make-do event. The tree was decorated with natural materials gathered from the fields and woods. Leftover scraps of yarn, paper, string, and fabric were also put to use, and homemade food items added a special flavor to the tree.

You can make ornaments from corn husks, nuts, feathers, cones, pods, grasses, and dried flowers along with fabric scraps of calico, gingham, burlap, denim, and muslin. Warm earth colors may be used to duplicate the natural, muted dyes made from berries, roots, onion skins, barks, and such.

Homemade sugar cookies, corn-husk baskets filled with nuts, popcorn chains, knitted mittens and stockings can be attached to the tree. On the frontier, functional gifts, lovingly and patiently made by hand, were exchanged.

If you are fortunate to possess a patchwork or appliqué quilt, it could be placed at the base of the tree to reinforce the fresh, honest, unaffected frontier look.

CORN-HUSK DOLLS

In the seventeenth century, American colonists from Europe saw corn for the first time, growing in Indian villages. Most likely, the Indians taught these early settlers how to make corn-husk dolls. Considering that corn was a main food, and that the resourceful colonists were forced by circumstances to waste nothing, it seems likely that the corn-husk doll was one of America's first toys.

The corn-husk doll is also a tradition in Czechoslovakia and Mexico.

MATERIALS AND TOOLS

Dried corn husks
Straight pins
Ruler
Scissors
Button or carpet thread
Pipe cleaners
White glue—clear-drying
Corn silk, string, embroidery thread, or crewel yarn
   for hair
Felt pen—black, permanent, fine-tipped
Raffia (optional)
Bobby pins
Nylon fishing line for hanging

HOW TO MAKE

1. Dip dried husks in warm water for about 15 minutes to make them pliable. Drain and wrap in a towel until ready to use. Always work with damp husks. If you are unable to complete the doll in one sitting, the entire doll can be re-dampened and finished later.

2. To make a head, form a ball the size of a marble from tightly wrapped strips of husks. Use a straight pin to hold the last end in place.

3. Cut a corn husk strip 3 x 6 inches and tie it in the center with thread (fig. 1).

4. Attach the tied strip to the center of the head, covering the head completely. Tie at the bottom to form a neck (fig. 2).

5. To make the arms, cut a 6-inch length of pipe cleaner. Bend the ends inward $\frac{1}{2}$ inch to form hands. Lay the pipe cleaner on a 1 x 6-inch strip of husk. Turn the ends of the husk over the hands, then roll the husk tightly around the pipe cleaner. Tie securely at the wrists with thread (fig. 3).

6. For each sleeve, place a $2\frac{1}{2}$ x 4-inch piece of husk $1\frac{1}{2}$ inches from the end of one of the hands and let it extend out beyond the hand (fig. 4).

7. Gather the husk around the arm and tie with thread (fig. 5).

8. Pull the extended husk back over the arm shaping a puffed sleeve and tie as shown (fig. 6).

9. To make the bodice, wrap the excess husk from the head over the arms; tie together under the arms (fig. 7).

10. Cut four 2 x 4-inch husk strips. Wrap 2 of them over each shoulder of the doll, crossing them in the front and the back. Pleat the husks across the shoulders. Tie the strips at the waist with thread (fig. 8).

11. To make the skirt, use 3 large husks. Position the doll's arms above her head. Tie the narrow ends around the waist: Because the husks will be pulled down over this tie to form the skirt, most of the husk should be above the tie. Once tied, pull the husks down to form the skirt.

12. Bend the torso, arms, and head into a lifelike position before the husks dry. Set the damp doll over a glass to support it while drying.

13. When dry, glue on crewel yarn, embroidery thread, string, or corn silk for hair. Keep the facial features simple: Add just 2 black dots for eyes, using a fine-tipped felt pen.

14. You may want to decorate your doll further by having her wear glasses, a cape, or flowers in her hair. She could hold a candle, bundles, sheet music, embroidery hoop, musical instrument, book, rolling pin, or a tiny basket. Below are directions for making some other accessories:

Apron—cut a curved edge along the top of a wide husk for the bottom of an apron. Gather the straight edge of the husk to the waist. Wrap a narrow strip of husk around the waist to cover the rough edges and tie in a bow at the back.

Shawl—drape a long husk over the shoulders and tie the ends in front.

Kerchief—cut a strip 2 inches wide, pin to the top of the head, and then gather it at the back of the neck. Tie the gathers together with a narrow strip of husk or a length of raffia (fig. 9).

Umbrella—use a wooden skewer, lollipop stick, or a thin wooden dowel for a handle. Cut a 2 x 4-inch husk. Keeping the 2-inch edge at the bottom, wrap the husk around the stick. Tie a narrow strip of husk or length of raffia around the top of the stick and one around the bottom (fig. 10).

Broom—use a wooden skewer, lollipop stick, tree twig, or a thin wooden dowel for a handle. Cut two 2 x 4-inch pieces of husks. Fringe along the 4-inch sides and roll around the handle. Tie in place with a narrow strip of husk, string, or length of raffia (fig. 11).

Bucket—roll a 2-inch-wide strip into a cylinder about ¾ inch in diameter. Hold in place with a pin until dry. Cut a circular bottom from a husk and a ⅛ x 3-inch strip for a handle. When dry, glue to the bucket (fig. 12).

Purse—cut a circle 4 inches in diameter; gather and tie with a narrow strip of husk or a length of raffia (fig. 13).

Hat—cut a circle 2½ inches in diameter from a husk. Pin to top of head to hold while wrapping a narrow strip of husk or length of raffia around the crown, forming a bow in the back. When dry, glue small dried flowers to the crown (fig. 14).

Basket—cut a 1½ x 2¼-inch oval from a doubled husk. Let dry, then glue the layers together. Cut a ½ x 3-inch strip and fold it over to measure ¼ inch wide. Clamp with bobby pins until dry. Bend up the sides of the basket and glue ends of the handle to it. Clamp with bobby pins until dry (fig. 15).

15. Thread a length of nylon fishing line or raffia through the back of the doll and tie to make a loop for hanging.

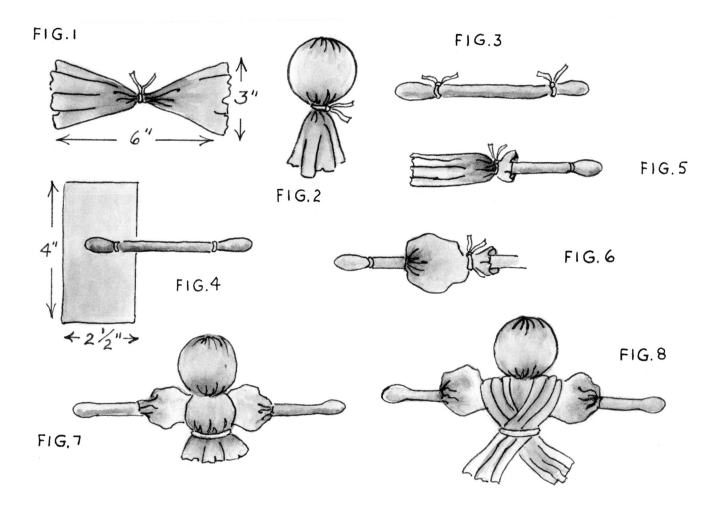

FIG.1

FIG.2

FIG.3

FIG.4

FIG.5

FIG.6

FIG.7

FIG.8

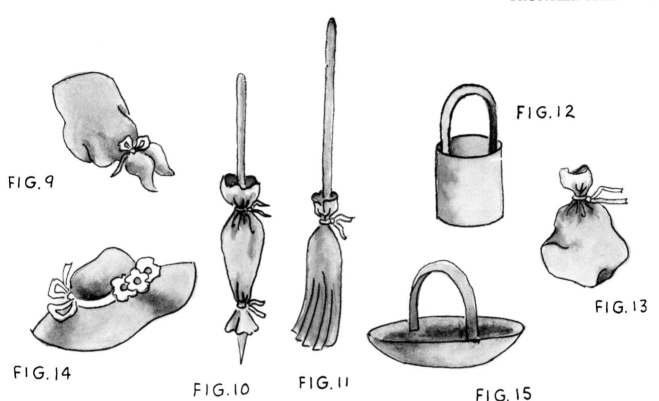

FIG. 9

FIG. 14

FIG. 10

FIG. 11

FIG. 12

FIG. 13

FIG. 15

CORN-HUSK ROSE

The first pioneers came to the Southern Appalachian mountains in the beginning of the eighteenth century. Today, as in the past, the physical isolation of the people living in this area of the United States makes it necessary for them to make what they need from readily available materials. Because of the increased interest in American folk crafts in recent years, many of these same products are now also being made for sale to the very large folk art markets outside Appalachia.

MATERIALS AND TOOLS

Dried corn husks—about 10 for each rose
Ruler
Florist's wire—22 gauge for stem
Button or carpet thread
Fabric dye—green
Cardboard for patterns
Pencil
Scissors
Florist's tape—green

HOW TO MAKE

1. Soak about 8 husks for the rose petals and about 2 husks for the leaves in warm water for about 15 minutes. Drain and wrap in a towel until ready to use. The husks must remain damp and pliable while working.

2. Fold a 10-inch length of florist's wire in half to make a stem. To make the center of the rose, make a small, tight knob from corn husk scraps and place it over the folded tip of the wire stem. Tie it securely

at the base with thread (fig. 1).

3. Enlarge the patterns to make cardboard templates for the petals and leaves (fig. 2). Trace around the templates onto husks to make 16 petals and 3 leaves, keeping the grain of the husk running the length of the petal. Cut out.

4. Curl the tip of each petal around your finger so it will bend in the desired direction before positioning it around the base. After spacing a few of the petals evenly around the base, tie thread around the base to hold the petals in place. Continue layering the petals, tying when needed. When all the petals are in place, tie more thread to keep them securely rooted at the base (fig. 3).

5. To color the leaves green, mix ¾ teaspoon of green fabric dye into 2 cups of boiling water. Dip the leaves completely so that they color evenly. When the desired color is reached (about 5 minutes), remove and rinse. Cut a jagged edge around each leaf.

6. Holding the 3 leaves around the base of the rose, tape them to the base with green florist's tape. Continue to wrap all exposed thread, petal and leaf ends, and stem with florist's tape.

7. Attach the corn-husk rose to the Christmas tree by bending the stem around a tree branch.

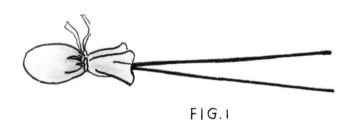

FIG.1

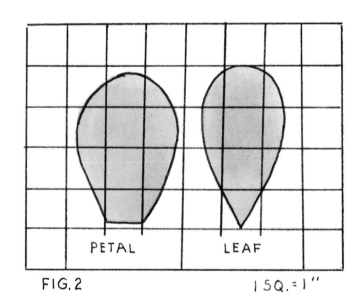

PETAL   LEAF

FIG. 2   1 SQ.= 1"

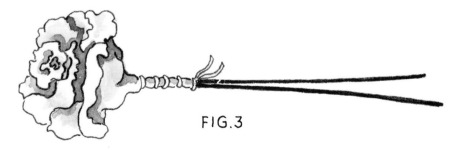

FIG.3

CORN-HUSK BASKET

Baskets for storing, gathering, drying, and carrying items to and from market have been made from all sorts of natural materials in all parts of the world.

The Pennsylvania Dutch took great care in making special Christmas baskets for their children. These baskets were hung upon the Christmas tree loaded with candies and nuts.

MATERIALS AND TOOLS

Dried corn husks
Ruler
Scissors
Needle
Button or carpet thread

HOW TO MAKE

1. Soak dried corn husks in warm water about 15 minutes, or until pliable. Drain and wrap in a towel until ready to use. Keep husks damp while working.
2. Cut husks into long, ½-inch-wide strips.
3. Sew 3 long husks of uneven lengths together at one end (fig. 1). Braid the 3 strips. When each of the 3 strips becomes too short for braiding, add an additional strip under the strip you want to lengthen and continue braiding. Continue this way until the braid is about 4 feet long.
4. To make the bottom of the basket, sew the damp braid with heavy thread, coiling tightly as you go, making a flat spiral mat about 2 inches in diameter (fig. 2).
5. When the base is large enough, set the next round of braid on edge (upright) instead of flat. Sew the upright braid to the base. Continue coiling and sewing the upright braid to build up the sides (fig. 3).
6. Braid 3 corn-husk strips to make a 6-inch length for the handle. Sew the braided handle to the sides of the basket.
7. This makes a very small basket. Fill it with white jelly bean "eggs" for a miniature egg basket.
8. Hang the basket by its handle.

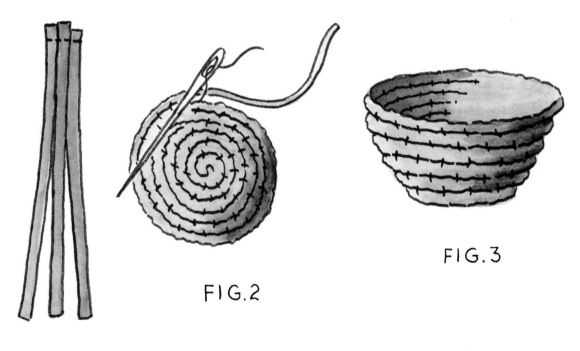

FIG.1

FIG.2

FIG.3

CORN-HUSK HAT

MATERIALS AND TOOLS

Dried corn husks
Ruler
Scissors
Needle
Button or carpet thread
Narrow ribbon for hat band
Nylon fishing line for hanging

HOW TO MAKE

1. Soak dried corn husks in warm water about 15 minutes, until pliable. Drain and wrap in a towel until ready to use. Keep husks damp while working.

2. Cut husks into long, ½-inch-wide strips. Sew 3 strips together at one end (fig. 1). Braid the 3 strips and sew the ends together. Repeat until you have enough braided strips to make the size hat you desire.

3. To make the top of the crown, wind a braid in a circle, stitching the braid together as you wind. Add as many braids you need to make the size hat you want (fig. 2).

4. To make the side of the crown, add a braid down from the edge of the top of the crown, stitching the braid together as you wind. Make the side of the crown as high as you want by sewing several braided strips together (fig. 3).

5. To make the brim, wind and sew a braid out from the bottom edge of the crown. Make the brim as wide as you want by sewing several braided strips together (fig. 4).

6. Wrap a narrow ribbon band around the crown of the hat and stitch to secure.

7. Thread a length of nylon fishing line through the edge of the brim and tie to make a loop for hanging.

FIG. 1

FIG. 2

FIG. 3

FIG. 4

POPCORN CHAIN

Corn was not known in Europe at the time the first European settlers arrived in America. They ate corn for the first time when the Indians gave them popped corn as a token of friendship and kindness. Popcorn is genuinely an American contribution to the Christmas tree.

MATERIALS AND TOOLS

Popped corn
Darning needle
Heavy thread or thin string

HOW TO MAKE

1. Make popcorn, preferably 2 weeks before string-ing so that it will have time to soften.

2. Thread a needle with a 4-foot length of thread or string and knot the end. Push the needle through the popped corn, pull the corn back along the thread, then keep adding pieces. Tie several 4-foot lengths together before placing the chain around the tree.

MOUNTAIN WHEEL STAR

MATERIALS AND TOOLS

$\frac{3}{4}$-inch pine (12- or 18-inch length)
Vise
Wood plane
Ruler
Scissors
White glue—clear-drying
Paper clips or bobby pins
Nylon fishing line for hanging

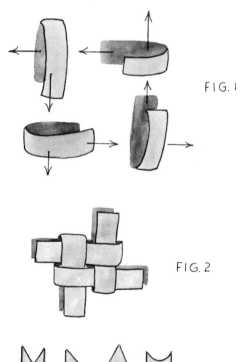

FIG. 1

FIG. 2

HOW TO MAKE

1. Soak a piece of $\frac{3}{4}$-inch pine in water at least 8 hours, then place in a vise and plane off thin shavings. Keep the shavings damp while you are working so they will remain pliable.

2. Cut the $\frac{3}{4}$-inch-wide shavings into several 6-inch-long strips.

3. Fold four 6-inch-long strips in half. Weave the folded strips as shown (figs. 1 and 2).

4. Cut the 4 ends of the star in one of the ways shown (fig. 3).

5. Place a small amount of glue in the folds to hold the star together. Let dry between paper towels and weight down.

6. Thread a length of nylon fishing line through one of the folds and tie to make a loop for hanging.

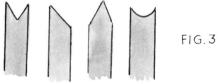

FIG. 3

PATCHWORK ORNAMENTS

On the American frontier, winter was the time to stay home and make all sorts of things from bits and pieces, snippets and swatches of frugally saved fabric. It was a way of recycling expensive printed and colored imported fabrics. Patchwork also served as an outlet for the pioneer woman's creative longings. The first American quilts were traditionally made of scraps.

Star

The star, a favorite motif, was not only used for patchwork quilt designs, but for cookie cutters, barn decorations, and other articles as well. The star is also a universal Christmas symbol, used to decorate greeting cards, trees, gifts, and all sorts of Christmas items. It represents the Star in the East that led the Wise Men to the baby Jesus.

MATERIALS AND TOOLS

Cardboard or thin plastic lid for template
Pencil
Scissors
Fabric scraps—preferably cotton, in a variety of small patterned prints and solid colors
Straight pins
Needle
Thread
Polyester fiberfill
Nylon fishing line for hanging
Ruler

HOW TO MAKE

1. Make a diamond-shaped template for the star by tracing the actual size pattern onto cardboard or plastic lid (fig. 1). Cut out.

2. Trace around the template onto fabric scraps to make 12 diamond shapes. The pattern includes a ¼-inch seam allowance. Cut out.

3. With right sides facing, pin and stitch 6 diamonds together, one at a time, to make a front (fig. 2). Do the same with the other 6 diamonds to make a back. Press all seams in one direction.

4. Sew the star halves together, right sides facing, with a ¼-inch seam allowance, leaving an opening for turning. Turn right-side-out. Stuff firmly with fiberfill and stitch the opening closed.

5. Sew a loop of nylon fishing line to the star for hanging.

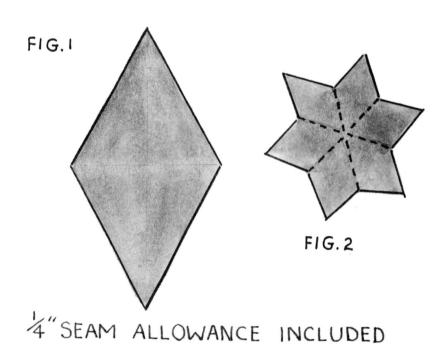

FIG. 1

FIG. 2

¼" SEAM ALLOWANCE INCLUDED

Triangle Tree

The materials and tools are the same as for the Star.

HOW TO MAKE

1. Make templates for the tree by tracing the enlarged, actual-size patterns onto cardboard or plastic lids (figs. 3 and 4). Cut out.

2. Trace around the triangle template onto fabric scraps to make 6 triangular shapes. Cut out.

3. With right sides facing and using ¼-inch seam allowances, pin and stitch 2 triangles together, leaving 1 side open for turning. Turn right-side-out. Stuff lightly with fiberfill and stitch the opening closed. Do the same with the other 4 triangles to make a total of 3 stuffed triangles. These will become the "foliage" of the tree.

4. Enlarge the square to the dimensions shown to make a paper pattern. Cut out 2 fabric square shapes, using the paper pattern as a guide.

5. With right sides facing, pin and stitch the 2 squares together, leaving ¼-inch seam allowances and one side open for turning. Turn right-side-out. Stuff lightly with fiberfill and stitch the opening closed. This will become the "trunk" of the tree.

6. Stitch the point of each stuffed triangle to the center back of another. Sew the stuffed square to the bottom triangle to complete the tree (fig. 5).

7. Sew a loop of nylon fishing line to the top of the tree for hanging.

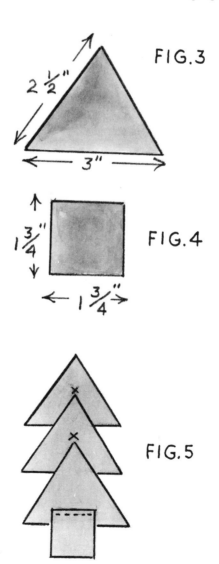

FIG.3

2 ½"

3"

FIG.4

1 ¾"

1 ¾"

FIG.5

Yo-Yo Tree

Another way to use fabric scraps to make ornaments is to adopt the clever technique the pioneer women used to make "Yo-Yo" Quilts. These quilts, sometimes called Flower Garden Quilts or Pom-Pom Quilts, were not made for warmth but rather for beauty and were used as spreads.

The materials and tools are the same as for the Star; in addition, you will need a compass.

HOW TO MAKE

1. Make a template for the yo-yos by cutting a circle 2½ inches in diameter from cardboard or a plastic lid.

2. Trace around the template, then cut 6 circles from fabric scraps.

3. To make each yo-yo, turn under the raw edge of the circle and run a line of basting/gathering stitches along the edge through the 2 thicknesses. Pull the gathering thread to draw the edges to the center; then tie off the thread in a double knot. Flatten the fabric into a 1-inch circle (fig. 6).

4. Turn the yo-yos over, and stitch each yo-yo to adjoining yo-yos where they touch (fig. 7). This will become the "foliage" of the tree.

5. Make a template for the "trunk" of the tree by cutting a 1¾-inch square from cardboard or a plastic lid. Trace onto fabric to make 2 square shapes. Cut out.

6. With right sides facing, pin and stitch the 2 squares together, leaving ¼-inch seam allowances and 1 side open for turning. Turn right-side-out. Stuff lightly with fiberfill and stitch the opening closed.

7. Sew the stuffed square to the yo-yos to complete the tree ornament (fig. 8).

8. Sew a loop of nylon fishing line to the top of the tree for hanging.

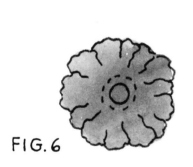

FIG. 6

FIG. 7

FIG. 8

Yo-Yo Wreath

The materials and tools are the same as for the Star; in addition, you will need a compass, ruler, and a ⅜-inch wide ribbon bow.

HOW TO MAKE

1. Make a template for the yo-yos by cutting a circle 2½ inches in diameter from cardboard or a plastic lid.

2. Trace, then cut 17 circles from fabric scraps.

3. To make each yo-yo, turn under the raw edge of the circle and run a line of basting/gathering stitches along the edge through the two thicknesses. Place a wad of fiberfill in the center; then pull the gathering thread tightly to draw the edge to the center. Tie off the thread in a double knot.

4. Sew a double strand of thread through the centers of each of the 17 stuffed yo-yos and pull tightly to form a circular wreath, allowing the edges to plump. Knot the ends of the thread to hold the yo-yos securely in place (fig. 9).

5. Stitch a ribbon bow to the wreath. Sew a loop of nylon fishing line to the top of the wreath for hanging.

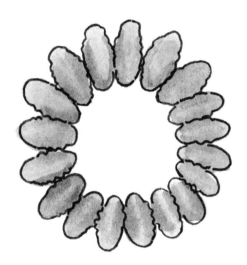

FIG. 9

ORNAMENTS FROM NATURAL MATERIALS

Listed below are some natural materials that can be used to make dolls, birds, and wreaths. These can be found in grocery stores, foreign and health-food shops, animal-feed shops, florists' or florist supply stores, in the woods and countryside, or in your own backyard.

Nuts—acorns, hickory nuts, chestnuts, walnuts, pecans, pistachio nuts, almonds, hazel nuts, peanuts, filbert nuts

Cones—pine, larch, hemlock, fir

Pods—milkweed, eucalyptus, goldenrod, oriental poppy, iris, yucca, rose hips

Seeds and Beans—sunflower, squash, cantaloupe, tomato, apple, grapefruit, cherry pits, pumpkin, white navy beans, dried peas

Vines—jasmine, grape, eucalyptus, ivy, birch, honeysuckle, bougainvillea

Dried plants and flowers

Feathers

Dolls

On the frontier, fancy dolls were virtually nonexistent. A factory-made doll from Europe would have to travel by boat, then by stagecoach and horseback to reach the homes on the distant frontier. The inventive frontier mother fashioned "make-do" dolls for her children from materials she found in the woods and fields, along with treasured scraps of cloth.

The word "doll" was first used about 1750. There was no such word in earlier days. In the American colonies what we call "dolls" were called "babes" or "babies" and "little ladies."

MATERIALS AND TOOLS

See list of Natural Materials on page 13.

White glue—clear-drying
Felt pen—black, permanent, fine-tipped
Scissors
Fabric scraps
Needle
Thread
Tiny rickrack
Colored chenille stems
Nylon fishing line for hanging

HOW TO MAKE

1. Glue a small nut such as an acorn to the top of a small pine cone to make a head and a body. Dried grass can be glued to the nut for hair.

2. Paint 2 black dots on the nut for eyes with a black felt pen.

3. To make a skirt, hem along one long edge of a rectangular piece of fabric scrap, then fold the fabric in half, right sides together, and stitch the two short sides together. Turn right-side-out. Turn under the remaining raw edge and baste. Slip the skirt over the pine cone, pull the basting thread to gather the skirt around the cone, exposing a few scales, and tie in a knot. Glue rickrack trim around the bottom of the skirt.

4. Cut a piece of fabric for an apron. Hem the bottom and the sides. Turn under the raw top edge of the apron and baste. Pull the basting thread to gather the apron around the doll's waist and tie at the back of the cone.

5. Cut a triangular piece of fabric for a kerchief and glue the long edge around the face.

6. To make arms, glue a length of colored chenille stem, cut to size, around the pine-cone body. Choose a color that complements the skirt fabric. You may prefer to sew fabric around the chenille stem before gluing it to the cone. If so, use a pink chenille stem. To make hands, turn up the ends of the chenille stem or glue tiny, hollow pods to the ends of the chenille stem (fig. 1).

7. To add interest, use your imagination to create an object made from natural materials for the doll to hold. Here are some suggestions: walnut shell basket, acorn cap bowl, bean or nut baby, bouquet of dried flowers or wheat sheaves, tiny vine wreath, string of dried berries, twig and dried grass broom, or a bundle of firewood.

8. Thread a loop of nylon fishing line through the top of the kerchief for hanging.

Birds

An old Christmas saying to bring good luck gives inspiration to make these little birds:

The best of life will come to thee
If a bird nests in your Christmas tree

MATERIALS AND TOOLS

See list of Natural Materials on page 13.

White glue—clear-drying
Feathers or pine-cone scales for wings and tail
Felt pen—black, permanent, fine-tipped
Nylon fishing line for hanging
Raffia
Needle with large eye
Scissors
Florist's wire—22 gauge

HOW TO MAKE

1. Glue a small pod, with the stem attached, to a nut. The pod becomes a head, the attached stem the beak, and the nut the body of a small bird (fig. 2).

2. Glue feathers or pine-cone scales to the body for wings and a tail. Let dry.

3. If no stem is attached to the pod head or you have used a nut for a head, glue on a paper beak (fig. 3).

4. Paint 2 small dots for eyes with a black felt pen.

5. Have the bird "fly" by attaching it to a length of nylon fishing line tied to a branch of the Christmas tree.

6. The bird could be glued inside a hollow pod or grass nest. To make a grass nest, wind lengths of dried grass into coils and attach one coil to the other by sewing them together with raffia (fig. 4).

7. To secure the nest to the tree, thread a length of florist's wire through the bottom of the nest, then bend the wire ends down and twist around the tree branch.

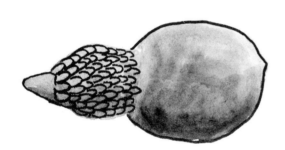

FIG. 1

FIG. 3

FIG. 2

FIG. 4

Wreaths

MATERIALS AND TOOLS

See list of Natural Materials on page 13.

White glue—clear-drying
Florist's wire—22 gauge
Nylon fishing line for hanging

HOW TO MAKE

1. Coil thin, supple vines into a tightly woven, compact wreath about 3 to 4 inches in diameter. Tie the wreath in 3 or 4 places with florist's wire to hold the vines in place. The number of vines to use will depend on the length and thickness of the vines.

2. Decorate the wreath base by gluing on an attractive arrangement of tiny cones, pods, nuts, and dried flowers.

3. Attach a loop of nylon fishing line at the top of the wreath for hanging.

AMERICAN GINGERBREAD MEN

American gingerbread men probably originated with German settlers who made edible gingerbread dolls to represent Saint Nicholas. In the early days, gingerbread men were popular Christmas decorations. Shop owners would sometimes give gingerbread men with the shop's name on them to children. This was not only an act of kindness but a clever gimmick for advertising as well.

INGREDIENTS

$\frac{1}{2}$ cup shortening
$\frac{1}{2}$ cup sugar
$\frac{1}{2}$ cup light molasses
$\frac{1}{2}$ tablespoon vinegar
1 beaten egg
3 cups sifted enriched flour
$\frac{1}{2}$ teaspoon soda
$\frac{1}{2}$ teaspoon cinnamon
$\frac{1}{2}$ teaspoon ginger
$\frac{1}{4}$ teaspoon salt
Seedless raisins (for eyes and buttons)

MATERIALS AND TOOLS

Gingerbread man cutter
Drinking straw
Nylon fishing line for hanging

HOW TO MAKE

1. Bring shortening, sugar, molasses, and vinegar to a boil. Cool. Add egg.
2. Sift the dry ingredients and add to the egg mixture. Mix well. Chill.
3. Roll out the dough $\frac{1}{4}$-inch thick on a lightly floured surface. Cut with a gingerbread man cutter.
4. Lift onto a greased cookie sheet with a wide spatula, placing gingerbread men 2 inches apart. Press raisins into the dough for eyes and buttons. Use a knife gently to make indentations in the dough for a smiling mouth, hands, and feet (fig. 1).
5. Use a drinking straw to make a hole at the top of each cookie for hanging.
6. Bake 12 to 15 minutes in a moderate oven (375° F) until lightly browned.
7. Thread a length of nylon fishing line through the hole and tie the ends to make a loop for hanging.

Yield: About $2\frac{1}{2}$ dozen cookies

FIG. 1

PENNSYLVANIA DUTCH GINGER COOKIES

In the early days, ginger cookies, cut into shapes of hearts, bells, angels, stars, tulips, birds, farm animals, etc., were baked by the "washbasket" full for Christmas sharing. Cookie cutters were brought out of storage from the previous Christmas, and cutters were loaned to neighbors. It was not uncommon for fifty or more different cookie cutter designs to be used by a single family for Christmas baking.

HOW TO MAKE

1. To make the dough, use the same ingredients and directions as for American Gingerbread Men.

2. Use cookie cutters or make cardboard patterns, cutting out dough around the patterns with a sharp knife. See Patterns for Cookies on page 138.

3. Use a drinking straw to make a hole in the top of each cookie for hanging.

4. After cookies cool, decorate them with Frosting Paints. See Frosting Paints under Grattimannen Cookies on page 131. Some of these cookies can also be decorated with Sprinkled Sugar Frosting (recipe follows).

5. Thread a length of nylon fishing line and tie ends to make a loop for hanging.

SPRINKLED SUGAR FROSTING

Brush the tops of the cookies lightly with corn syrup, then sprinkle with sugar tinted with food coloring. Let stand until sugar is set.

Yield: About 2½ dozen cookies

Collector's Early American Tree

You can fashion a unique and interesting Christmas tree to display imitation or authentic Early American collectibles. Place twiggy, bare branches in a crock, bucket, or wooden keg, holding them in place with stones. Or keep the same Christmas tree year after year, as was the frugal custom in earlier days. After the first Christmas, the tree was often stored to dry out. The next year it was stripped of its needles, and then pieces of white cotton batting were laid along its limbs and under the tree to simulate snow.

You can become familiar with the exciting history of America as you make Amish quilt ornaments, Pennsylvania Dutch hex signs, miniature weather vanes, "tin" quilt templates, and so forth. American folk art is really derived from the popular cultures of people of various nationalities who settled here.

Miniature doll-house furniture—such as chairs, tables, and chests—can be tied to the branches to duplicate the old-time peddler's or drummer's samples. Metal cookie cutters can be hung on the tree in imitation of the old-time cookie cutters made from scraps of tin by itinerant craftsmen. Old buttons, metal thimbles, homemade rag dolls, and animals can also be tied to the tree for added interest.

If you are a collector of Early American antiques, you can create unusual and interesting effects by displaying them on and under your tree.

WEATHERVANES

Weathervanes, recorded from the seventeenth century, are America's first sculptures. They were a necessity for the farmer, since they provided the means of determining wind direction, which was important for weather forecasting.

Common weathervanes included profiles of domestic animals (horses, cows, pigs, roosters, sheep), which adorned the barns, hen houses, and stables that housed them. Many of the earliest vanes were homemade forms cut or whittled from flat pine or other soft wood. Some were painted in solid colors, most frequently Indian red or yellow ochre.

After 1850 most weathervanes were manufactured.

MATERIALS AND TOOLS

Paper for pattern
Pencil
Scissors
$\frac{1}{8}$-inch plywood
Jigsaw or coping saw
Sandpaper
Paintbrush
Gesso
Acrylic paints
Turpentine
Linseed oil
Burnt umber oil paint
Rag
Drill with $\frac{1}{8}$-inch bit
Nylon fishing line for hanging

HOW TO MAKE

1. Enlarge and trace one of the suggested animal shapes onto paper to make a pattern (fig. 1). Cut out.

2. Trace around the paper pattern onto plywood. Then, carefully cut out the wooden animal, using a jigsaw or coping saw.

3. Round the edges with sandpaper.

4. Paint both sides of the animal with gesso to seal the wood. Let dry.

5. Paint the animal with acrylic paints, using lighter colors than you want on the finished piece—the antiquing process will darken the weathervane. Let dry.

6. Make a glazing liquid by thinning a small quantity of burnt umber paint with 3 parts turpentine to 1 part linseed oil.

7. "Antique" by applying the glaze liberally with a paint brush. Using a rag, wipe some off while it is still wet: more at the center, less at the ends. If you don't like the way it looks, you can remove it while it's wet, with turpentine.

8. Drill a hole, using a $\frac{1}{8}$-inch drill bit, at the top of the animal for hanging. See the X on the pattern for placement of hole.

9. Thread a length of nylon fishing line through the hole and tie ends to make a loop.

FIG.1

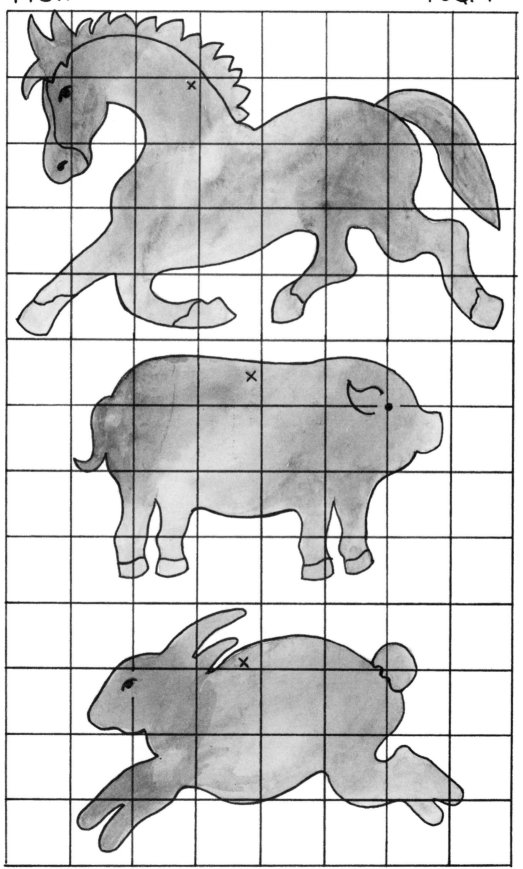

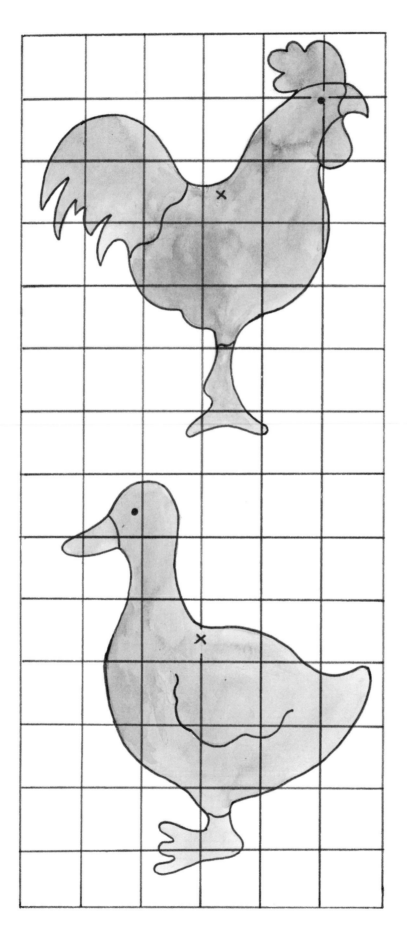

1 SQ. = 1"

I SQ. = I "

"HOMESPUN" BARNYARD ANIMALS

The making of cloth was such a long and laborious process for the frontier woman that worn clothing was not discarded but reused in a number of ways. Wool from sheep had to be sheared, washed, combed, and carded before it was spun into yarn. Thread made from flax was also prepared. The thread and yarn then had to be colored with dyes made from leaves, bark, berries, onion skins, and roots to get various colors before being woven into cloth on a loom. Clothing was chiefly made of linsey-woolsey, a cloth part linen, part wool.

MATERIALS AND TOOLS

Paper for patterns
Pencil
Straight pins
Scissors
Gingham fabric in checks or plaids and other fabrics
   with grid patterns
Needle
Thread
Crochet hook (optional)
Polyester fiberfill
Yarn

HOW TO MAKE

1. Enlarge and trace one or all of the animal shapes onto paper (fig. 1). Cut out.

2. Pin the paper pattern onto gingham fabric that has been folded in half, right sides together. Cut out.

3. With the right sides facing, sew the 2 fabric pieces together, leaving ¼-inch seam allowance and a 1-inch opening to allow for stuffing.

4. Snip *V*'s around the curved edges, then turn right-side-out.

5. Stuff the animal with fiberfill. A crochet hook is handy for reaching tiny places. Stitch the opening closed.

6. Hand-sew the edges with an overcast stitch (fig. 2).

7. Add a yarn tail or mane, depending upon the animal, and a length of looped yarn for hanging.

SEAM ALLOWANCE INCLUDED   1 SQ. = 1"   FIG. 1

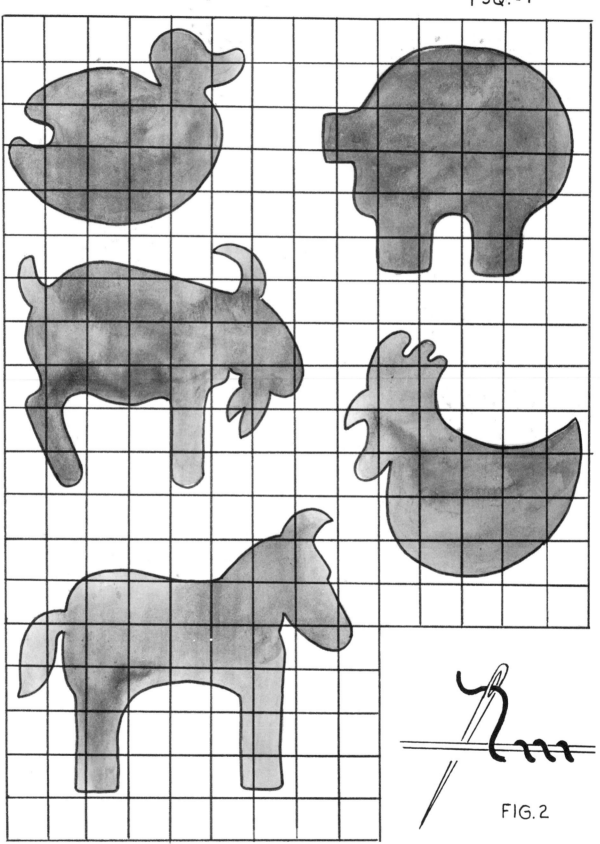

1 SQ. = 1″

FIG. 2

SIOUX INDIAN RAG DOLL

Rag dolls are the most popular of all homemade dolls. The unbreakable, huggable, humble rag doll has been loved by children throughout history. One of the oldest rag dolls was used in Egypt about 2,000 years ago.

This Sioux Indian doll, made entirely of fabric scraps, is a favorite traditional doll of the Sioux Indians of South Dakota.

MATERIALS AND TOOLS

Fabric scraps—white and assorted colors
Ruler
Scissors
String or heavy thread for tying
Needle
Sewing thread
Small safety pin
Nylon fishing line for hanging

HOW TO MAKE

1. To make the head and body, crush an 8-inch square of solid, light-colored fabric into a ball. Drop another 8-inch square of the same cloth over this and tightly tie around the neck with string or heavy thread.

2. Drape a 7-inch square of folded, dark cloth over part of the head, exposing the face, and tie at the neck with string or heavy thread.

3. Make the dress from a 5 x 10-inch piece of fabric folded into a square. Cut each side up at a slight angle toward the fold, then out to the edge to make sleeves. Sew the side seams and hem around the bottom of the dress (fig. 1).

4. Cut a hole in the fold to fit tightly over the doll's head. Place the dress over the doll's head. Cut away any excess material that may be hanging below the dress.

5. Make a shawl from a 7-inch square of fabric. Fold it into a triangle, then place it around the doll's shoulders and fasten it in front with a small safety pin. No facial features are placed on this doll.

6. Sew a loop of nylon fishing line to the top of the head for hanging.

FIG. 1

WOOD SHAVING CHAIN

MATERIALS AND TOOLS

¾-inch pine (12- or 18-inch length)
Vise
Wood plane
Ruler
Scissors
White glue—clear-drying
Paper clips or bobby pins

HOW TO MAKE

1. Soak a piece of ¾-inch pine in water at least 8 hours, then place in a vise and plane off thin shavings.

Keep the shavings damp while you are working so they will remain pliable.

2. Cut the ¾-inch-wide shavings into several 6-inch-long strips.

3. Roll 1 of the strips into a circle, slightly overlapping the ends. Glue ends to secure. Hold in place with a paper clip or bobby pin. Insert another strip through the first, roll into a circle, secure with glue, and hold in place with a paper clip or bobby pin. Continue in this manner until you have a long chain to drape around the tree. Let dry before removing the paper clips or bobby pins.

AMISH QUILT ORNAMENTS

The Amish, referred to as "the plain people," settled in Pennsylvania in the 1720's. Amish women in Pennsylvania, Ohio, and Indiana communities have since become well-known as makers of distinctive quilts. Their boldly colored quilts are in sharp contrast to their plain, somber dress. Their quilts remind one of large, modern, abstract paintings, with glowing colors of mulberry, tobacco brown, black, red, and medium and slate blue sewed into geometric shapes.

The Amish still reject material luxuries and teach separation from the world. They do not put up Christmas trees. Nor do they have a Santa Claus, because they would consider that lying to their children. Instead, they have the custom of "setting plates." Children place their plates on the kitchen table Christmas Eve and on Christmas morning find gifts from their Moms and Dads on the plate.

MATERIALS AND TOOLS

Felt—in traditional colors of mulberry,
    tobacco brown, black, red, and medium
    and slate blue
Paper
Pencil
Ruler
Scissors
Pins
White glue—clear-drying
Needle
Thread
Polyester fiberfill
Ribbon—⅜-inch-wide for hanging

HOW TO MAKE

1. For each ornament, cut two 4-inch squares of felt in colors used by the Amish (or similar colors).

2. Enlarge the design shapes for one or more of the motifs to make paper patterns (fig. 1). Cut out. Pin the patterns to felt pieces that contrast in color with the squares and cut out. Glue the design shapes to one of the 4-inch squares of felt.

3. Use a running stitch to stitch the two 4-inch squares of felt together. See fig. 2 for Indian Mirrored Cloth Figures, on page 88. Leave a ¾-inch opening for stuffing.

4. Stuff the ornament with fiberfill. Insert a loop of ⅜-inch-wide ribbon for hanging and stitch the opening closed.

FIG. 1

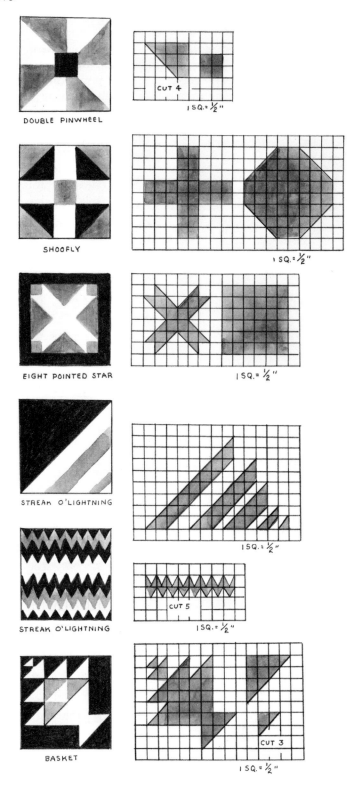

DOUBLE PINWHEEL

CUT 4

1 SQ. = ½"

SHOOFLY

1 SQ. = ½"

EIGHT POINTED STAR

1 SQ. = ½"

STREAK O'LIGHTNING

1 SQ. = ½"

STREAK O'LIGHTNING

CUT 5

1 SQ. = ½"

BASKET

CUT 3

1 SQ. = ½"

"TIN" QUILT TEMPLATES

These ornaments are adaptations of tin templates used in the nineteenth century for appliqué quilt animal patterns. Templates were made in the exact size and shape of the finished piece, then laid on the wrong side of the fabric and traced around with chalk or pencil. The piece was then cut out following the lines but leaving margins to be folded underneath like seam allowances. Appliqué quiltmakers favored plain-colored or small-print fabrics and often stylized their subjects. Early templates were also made from paper, cardboard, and wood.

MATERIALS AND TOOLS

Paper—for patterns
Pencil
Stiff aluminum foil—disposable baking sheets sold in grocery stores or foil containers from TV dinners or frozen pies
Masking tape
Ballpoint pen
Manicure scissors
Liquid black shoe polish
Steel wool
Needle—to punch hole for hanging
Nylon fishing line—for hanging

HOW TO MAKE

1. Enlarge and trace one or more of the suggested animal shapes onto paper to make a pattern (fig. 1).

2. Attach the paper pattern to a sheet of stiff aluminum foil with masking tape. Lightly trace around the pattern with a ballpoint pen, leaving a slight impression on the foil.

3. Remove the paper pattern and use manicure scissors to cut the animal shape from the foil, using the impression to guide you.

4. Cover the surface of the foil animal with a coat of liquid black shoe polish. Let dry.

5. Use a piece of steel wool to shine and give the "tin" a worn, antique appearance.

6. Repeat steps 4 and 5 for the other side of the foil.

7. Use a needle to pierce a hole at the top of the ornament. Thread a length of nylon fishing line through the hole and tie ends to form a loop for hanging.

FIG.1

1 SQ. = 1"

PENNSYLVANIA DUTCH HEX SIGNS

Hex signs are found on the barns of the Pennsylvania Dutch, whose forefathers came to America in the 1600's and 1700's from the German Rhineland to seek religious freedom. Unlike the Amish and Mennonites, the Pennsylvania Dutch accept both the spiritual and material pleasures of the world. The bold, fresh colors used on their hex signs aptly express their joy of life.

Hex signs are made of wood and are often four to six feet in diameter. They are brightly painted with symbolic geometric designs incorporating hearts, stars, rosettes, tulips, birds, and other motifs. Their original purpose was to ward off evil spirits, but today they are used primarily for decoration.

The same decorative motifs used for hex signs can also be found on baptismal certificates, tombstones, tinware, furniture, quilts, and other articles made by the Pennsylvania Dutch.

MATERIALS AND TOOLS

Compass
Paper for pattern
Pencil
Scissors
Jigsaw or coping saw
⅛-inch plywood
Sandpaper
Paintbrush
Gesso
Carbon paper
Acrylic paints—assorted colors
Drill with ⅛-inch drill bit
Nylon fishing line—for hanging

HOW TO MAKE

1. Use a compass to make a paper pattern for a circle with a 3-inch diameter. Cut out.

2. Design a personal miniature hex sign on the paper pattern, using a combination of the Pennsylvania Dutch motifs suggested (fig. 1).

3. Using a jigsaw or coping saw, cut out a wooden circle with the same diameter as your paper pattern; then sand it to make a smooth, round edge.

4. Apply gesso to both sides of the wood to seal it. Let dry.

5. To transfer your hex sign to the wood, place a piece of carbon paper between the wood and your paper design, and then trace over the design with a pencil. Be careful not to press down on the rest of the carbon paper while you are tracing.

6. Paint the different areas of your design with acrylic paints in your choice of bright yellow, green, red, and blue. Accent the design with white. Let dry.

7. Drill a hole, using a ⅛-inch drill bit, at the top of the hex sign. Thread a length of nylon fishing line through the hole and tie ends together to form a loop for hanging.

FIG. 1

PINE-CONE ORNAMENT

When a pine cone is sliced lengthwise, the interior of the cone looks like a hand. In Sicily, it is believed that this hand symbolizes the hand of Jesus blessing the pine that hid Him and His mother from Herod's soldiers when they were escaping Egypt.

HOW TO MAKE

1. This process will brighten pine cones and give them a more attractive appearance for use as Christmas ornaments. Line a baking pan with foil. Place the cones on the pan and bake in 275° F oven for ½ hour. The sap will then coat and brighten the cones.

2. Tie each cone to the tree with a length of red yarn.

Contemporary Country Tree

Today, there is a nostalgic longing to "bring back the good old days," when life was supposedly simpler and less mechanical. This longing has inspired a revival of interest in the folk arts and crafts.

You can express this yearning for the past in a modern "back to basics" Christmas. Your tree can be trimmed with contemporary folk art ornaments that are whimsical interpretations of "country" while still keeping country flavor and mood. Use old designs and ideas in new ways to capture a fresh, crisp, updated country look.

BUSHEL AND BERRY BASKETS

These miniature duplications of a berry basket and a bushel basket, filled with candies imitating berries and other fruits and vegetables, will add a country touch to your tree. The candies can be purchased at specialty candy shops, or you can make your own from marzipan. (See Marzipan Candy on page 86.) You can also mold inedible fruits and vegetables from Celluclay to be used year after year in the baskets.

MATERIALS AND TOOLS

Soft wood such as pine (9 inches long, $\frac{3}{4}$- to 1-inch thick)
Vise
Wood plane
Small plastic-foam block
Waxed paper
Pencil
Ruler
Scissors
White glue—clear-drying
Straight pins
Bobby pins
Florist's wire—22 gauge for handles
Nylon fishing line—for hanging
Staples and staple gun (optional)

HOW TO MAKE

1. Soak a 9-inch-long, $\frac{3}{4}$- to 1-inch-thick soft piece of wood, such as pine, in water for at least 8 hours. Clamp the board in a vise and use a wood plane to cut several thin, 9-inch-long shavings. Soak the shavings in water about $\frac{1}{2}$ hour to make them pliable. These can be cut to size with scissors as you need them.

2. Prepare a working surface by covering a small plastic-foam block with waxed paper.

3. To make the bushel basket, cut 8 shavings into $\frac{1}{2}$ x 5-inch strips with scissors. Glue the strips, one over the other, in star fashion on the foam block. Push

a straight pin into the center of the crossed strips to secure them to the block (fig. 1).

4. Cut a $\frac{1}{4}$ x 9-inch strip to make an inside rim for the basket. Wrap the rim around the inside top of the basket by gently bending up each strip in the "star" and securing it to the rim with a dab of glue. Hold each strip in place with a bobby pin. Slightly overlap the ends of the rim (fig. 2). Remove the straight pin from the bottom of the basket.

5. Cut another $\frac{1}{4}$ x 9-inch strip to become an outside rim. Apply glue to one side of the strip; then wrap it around the outside of the basket in line with the inside rim. Lift, then replace each bobby pin as you go. Remove the bobby pins after the basket dries.

6. Shape 2 handles from thin florist's wire. Place a handle on each side of the basket by inserting the wire ends between the 2 rims. Glue to secure (fig. 3).

7. Tie nylon fishing line to the handles to make a loop for hanging.

8. To make the berry basket, cut 4 shavings into $\frac{3}{4}$ x 4-inch strips. Arrange the 4 strips on a foam block to make a woven center. Leave a small space between each strip. Secure the 4 corners with straight pins (fig. 4).

9. Cut a shaving to make a $\frac{1}{4}$ x $8\frac{1}{4}$-inch outside rim. Gently bend up each side and glue or staple to the rim. Slightly overlap the ends of the rim. If you choose to glue, hold the sides to the rim with bobby pins until the glue dries (fig. 5).

10. To hang, tie a length of nylon fishing line to each of the 4 corners of the basket; gather and tie together.

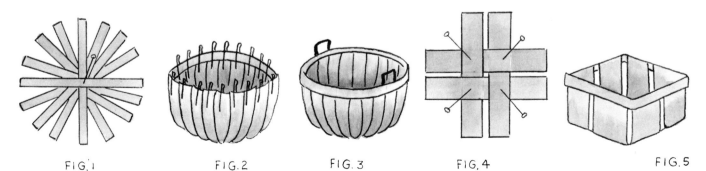

FIG. 1   FIG. 2   FIG. 3   FIG. 4   FIG. 5

APPLE

The apple is one of the oldest symbolic decorations for evergreen trees. In the Middle Ages apples were used as props for the Paradise Tree (see page 137). The accessible apple added color and fragrance to many of the early Christmas trees, as well as being a tasty treat.

MATERIALS AND TOOLS

Newspaper
Ruler
Masking tape
Waxed paper
Metylan Art Paste (or other mâché paste)
Paper toweling
Paper for leaf pattern
Pencil
Scissors
Gesso
Acrylic paints—red, green, brown
Paintbrush
Krylon Spray Fixative® (or other permanent protective coating)
Nylon fishing line for hanging

HOW TO MAKE

1. To make a mâché apple, crush a 14 x 23-inch piece of newspaper into the shape of an apple. Hold the apple-shape together with masking tape.

2. Working on waxed paper, tear paper toweling into ¾ x 2-inch strips and dip into mâché paste. Wring each strip by gently sliding it between 2 fingers, then smooth it over the apple. Cover the apple completely with at least 2 layers, slightly overlapping the strips. Dip a piece of paper toweling into the paste and tightly twist it into a stem about 1 inch long. Attach the stem to the apple with paste-covered strips. Let dry.

3. Make a paper pattern of the leaf (fig. 1). Lay the pattern on about 4 layers of paper toweling. Cut out. Keeping the layers together, dip into the paste and put the leaf aside on waxed paper to dry.

4. Apply a coat of gesso to the apple, stem, and leaf. Let dry.

5. Using acrylic paints, paint the apple red, the stem brown, and the leaf green. Let dry.

6. Glue the leaf to the apple.

7. Spray with a permanent protective coating.

8. Tie a length of nylon fishing line around the stem to make a loop for hanging.

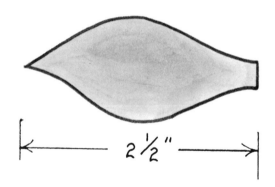

FIG. 1

2 ½ "

SCARECROW

With the assistance of science and technology, farmers today find it less difficult than in the past to keep the crows and ground hogs from damaging their crops. Fortunately, the amusing and supposedly frightening scarecrow can still be found in some rural areas.

A simple, wooden cross is the beginning of all scarecrows, but the similarity ends there. As cast-off clothing and other accessories are selected to clothe the scarecrow, it becomes a unique creation. The scarecrow is now being acknowledged as a form of folk sculpture.

MATERIALS AND TOOLS

$\frac{1}{4}$-inch wooden dowel
Ruler
Saw
Craft knife
White glue
Compass
Fabric scraps—white and other colors
Polyester fiberfill
Needle
Thread
Paper for patterns
Pencil
Straight pins
Raffia or straw—for stuffing and hat
Jute cord or string
Nylon fishing line for hanging

HOW TO MAKE

1. Cut two 6-inch lengths from a $\frac{1}{4}$-inch dowel to make a cross. In order to fit together, they will have to be notched. Cut a $\frac{1}{4}$-inch-wide notch in one of the 6-inch lengths of doweling beginning 2 inches from one end. Cut a similar notch midway in the other 6-inch dowel. Both notches should be about $\frac{1}{8}$-inch deep. Glue the 2 dowels together, forming a cross (fig. 1).

2. To make a head for the scarecrow, cut a circle with a 6-inch diameter of muslin or white fabric. Place fiberfill in the center of the fabric; then place it over the dowel at the top of the cross. Gather at the neck and tie with thread to secure (fig. 2).

3. Enlarge the clothing shapes to make paper patterns (fig. 3). Cut out.

4. Pin the shirt pattern onto printed fabric that has been folded in half (fig. 4). Cut out.

5. Using scissors, fringe the ends of the sleeves and the bottom of the shirt. Place the shirt on the scarecrow, right sides out, with the sleeves over the dowel. Sew the underside of the sleeves and the side seams. Fold over the shirt fabric at the neck and run a basting stitch around it. Pull the basting thread to gather the shirt around the neck. Stitch the shirt to the neck (fig. 5).

6. Stuff the shirt with raffia or straw, letting some of it stick out beyond the arms. Tie at the wrists with jute cord or string.

7. Pin the paper pattern for the pants to lightweight denim or other pant fabric that has been folded in half to make a front and a back. Cut out.

8. Fringe the bottom of each pant leg with scissors. With right sides facing, sew up the leg and side seams and hem around the waist. Turn right-side-out.

9. Pin the paper pattern for the bib and 2 suspenders to the same fabric as the pants and cut out. Hem the 3 sides of the bib, then sew to the top of the pants (fig. 6). Fold, then sew each suspender as shown (fig. 7). Sew the suspenders to the top of the bib (fig. 8).

10. Place the pants on the scarecrow with the wooden dowel inside one of the pant legs. Bring the suspenders up over the shoulders, crossing in back, and stitch to the waist at the back of the pants. Stuff the pants with raffia or straw, letting some of it stick out beyond the pant legs. Tie at the ankles with jute cord or string. Sew a tiny patch to one pant leg.

11. Pin the bandana pattern to fabric and cut out. Tie it around the neck.

12. To make the hat, tightly tie 6 long strands of raffia together with thread. Divide the strands into 3 groups (2 strands per group) and braid (fig. 9). Tie the end of the braid with thread to secure. Starting at the top of the crown, coil and sew the braid together, gradually working down the crown, widening it as you go. Continue coiling and sewing the braid together to make a wide flat brim extending out from the sides of the crown (fig. 10). Glue the hat to the head.

13. Thread a loop of nylon fishing line to the back of the scarecrow for hanging.

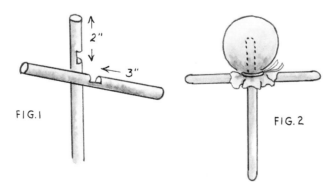

FIG.1

FIG.2

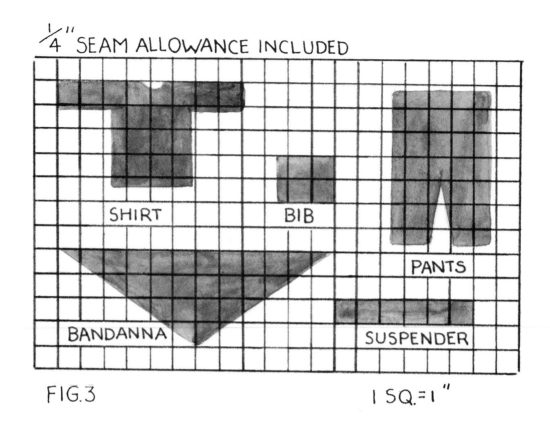

$\frac{1}{4}''$ SEAM ALLOWANCE INCLUDED

SHIRT

BIB

PANTS

BANDANNA

SUSPENDER

FIG. 3

1 SQ. = 1"

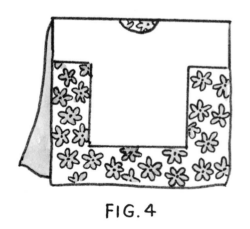

FIG. 4

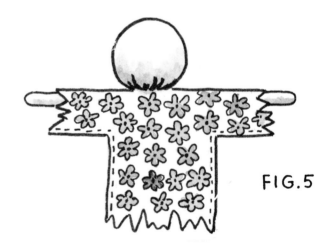

FIG. 5

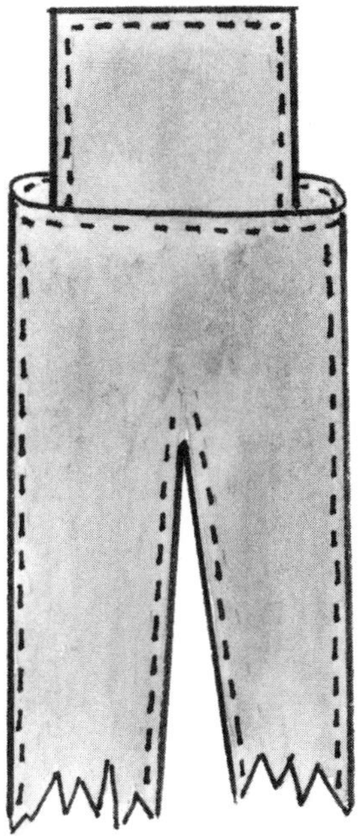

FIG. 6

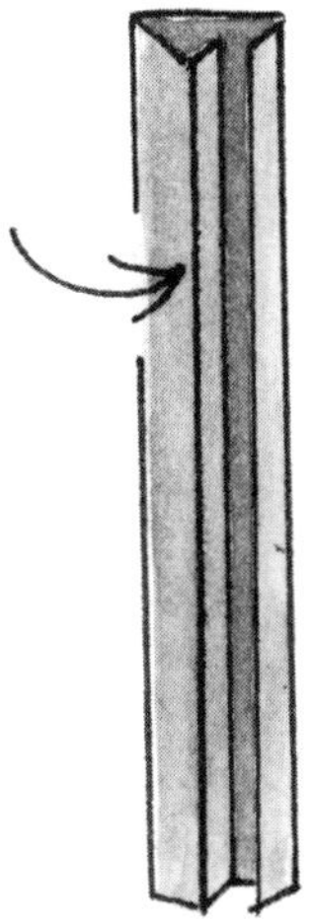

FIG. 7

FIG. 8

FIG. 9

FIG. 10

CONTEMPORARY COUNTRY WOODEN ORNAMENTS

Watermelon Slice—this slice of watermelon, seen nearly everywhere today, is a simple adaptation of the sculptured wooden watermelons created by Miles Carpenter, a contemporary folk artist.

Old-Time Skater's Stocking—this skater's stocking duplicates the old-time knitted stocking hung by the fireside in anticipation of Santa's arrival. The custom of hanging Christmas stockings originated from the story that long ago on Christmas Eve, St. Nicholas, squeezing his way down a chimney, accidentally dropped some gold coins. They fell into a stocking hung by the fireplace to dry, and since then, children look forward to Santa's filling each stocking with Christmas goodies and gifts.

Evergreen Tree—to many people the evergreen represents the tree of life, symbolizing Christ.

Country Home—decorate the doors and windows of this country home with the holiday spirit.

Sunbonnet—the functional sunbonnet protected a woman's face and neck when she did her gardening and other outdoor chores.

MATERIALS AND TOOLS

Paper for patterns
Pencil
Scissors
$\frac{1}{8}$-inch plywood
Jigsaw or coping saw
Sandpaper
Paintbrush
Gesso
Carbon paper
Acrylic paints
Drill with $\frac{1}{8}$-inch drill bit

HOW TO MAKE

1. Enlarge and trace the ornament shape you wish to make onto paper to make a paper pattern (fig. 1). Cut out.

2. Trace around the paper pattern onto plywood. Use a jigsaw or coping saw to cut the ornament out.

3. Smooth the edges with sandpaper.

4. To make the sunbonnet, see the separate directions under Sunbonnet that follow.

5. Paint both sides of the wood with gesso to seal. Let dry.

6. If you wish to decorate the ornament with the same design as illustrated, transfer the design to the wood by placing a piece of carbon paper between the wood and the paper design. Then trace over the design with a pencil. Be careful not to press down on the rest of the carbon paper while you are tracing.

7. Paint the ornament with acrylic paints. Let dry.

8. Drill a hole, using an $\frac{1}{8}$-inch drill bit, at the top of the ornament for hanging. See the X on the pattern for placement of hole.

FIG.1

1 SQ.= ½ "

Sunbonnet

For this ornament, you will need a piece of calico fabric, iron-on interfacing, rickrack, and white glue in addition to the materials and tools listed under the other contemporary country wooden ornaments.

HOW TO MAKE

1. Follow steps 1–3 for the other contemporary country wooden ornaments.

2. Enlarge and trace the bonnet shape (but not the "ribbon" dividing brim from crown) onto paper to make a paper pattern

3. Pin the paper pattern to a piece of folded calico fabric, and cut to make 2 bonnet shapes. Use the same pattern to cut 2 bonnet shapes from iron-on interfacing.

4. Iron the interfacing to the backs of the fabric pieces, and then glue the fabric to each side of the wooden sunbonnet, interfacing side down.

5. Using acrylic paints, paint the "ribbon" in a color that complements the calico fabric print. Let dry.

6. Glue rickrack or other trim to both sides of the sunbonnet.

7. Drill a hole using an $\frac{1}{8}$-inch drill bit at the top of the ornament for hanging. See the X on the pattern for placement of hole.

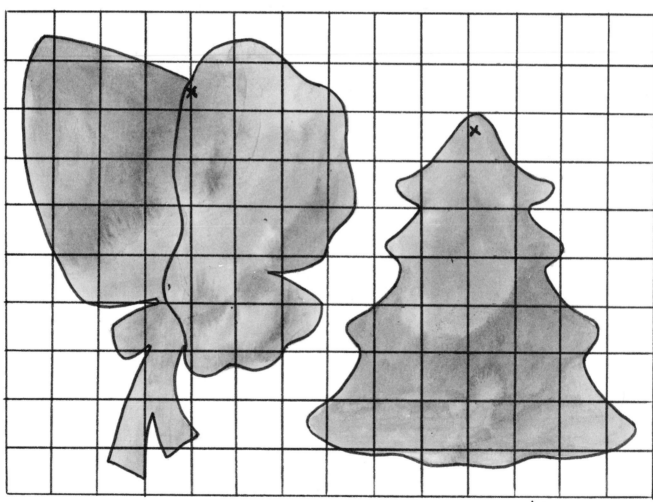

1 SQ. = $\frac{1}{2}$"

SUNBONNET ANGEL

This angel ornament is an adaptation of the Sunbonnet Baby design popular for appliqué quilts at the turn of the century and into the 'thirties and 'forties.

MATERIALS AND TOOLS

Plastic-foam ball—diameter about $1\frac{1}{4}''$
Plastic-foam bell—about 3" in length
Toothpick
White glue—clear-drying
Florist's wire—22 gauge for hanging ornament
Ruler
Waxed paper
Paper toweling
Metylan Art Paste (or other mâché paste)
Paper for patterns
Pencil
Scissors
Paintbrush
Gesso
Gold leaf enamel
Acrylic paints—assorted colors
Krylon Spray Fixative® (or other permanent protective coating)

HOW TO MAKE

1. The foam ball becomes the head of the angel and the foam bell becomes the body. Connect the ball to the bell by inserting one end of a glued toothpick into the ball and the other end of the glued toothpick into the top of the bell (fig. 1).

2. Insert the twisted ends of a loop of florist's wire into the bell for hanging the ornament after it is completed.

3. Working on waxed paper, cover the connected ball and bell with $\frac{3}{4}$ x 2-inch torn strips of paper toweling dipped in mâché paste. Slide each strip between two fingers to free it of any excess paste before smoothing it onto the ball and bell figure. Cover the figure completely, overlapping the strips. Apply at least 2 layers of strips, and then allow to dry.

4. Make paper patterns for the arms, wings, and bonnet by tracing the drawings (fig. 2). Place the patterns on 4 layers of paper toweling and cut out.

5. Place a wad of paste-covered paper toweling into the center of the bonnet back. Dip the bonnet into the paste and apply the bonnet to the back of the head. Gather the edges around the head (fig. 3).

6. Dip the bonnet brim into the paste; attach the straight edge to the bonnet, keeping the brim around and out from the face.

7. Dip the arms into the paste and shape them to the sides of the body, joining the hands together in front (fig. 4).

8. Dip the wings into the paste; attach the straight edges to each side of the back (fig. 5).

9. Stand the figure upright on the end of the bell until dry.

10. To make the ruffle for the dress, cut a 1 x 11-inch strip from 4 layers of paper toweling. Dip the ruffle into the paste, and then gather it around the bottom edge of the bell, letting the ruffle extend out from the bell (fig. 6). Turn the figure upside down in a glass to dry.

11. Apply a coat of gesso to the figure.

12. Paint the wings with gold leaf enamel.

13. Paint the rest of the figure with acrylic paints. Keep the painted facial features simple, and paint on hair. Design the "fabric" of the bonnet and dress with painted stripes, polka dots, small prints of flowers, hearts, or other motifs. Let dry.

14. Spray the angel with a permanent protective coating.

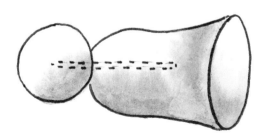

FIG. 1

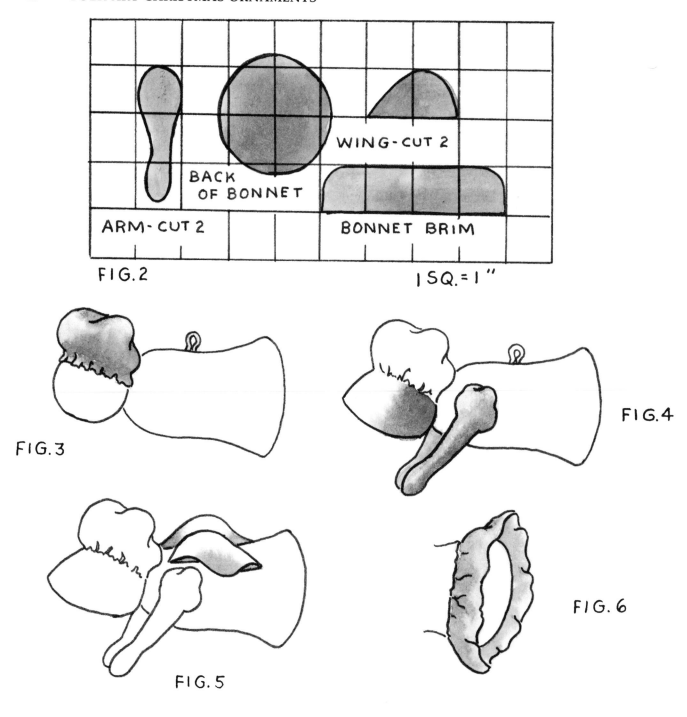

SNOWMAN

The snowman, which has been constructed for centuries around the world wherever snow is abundant, is now being recognized as a folk art form. Snowmen are as diverse as the people who create them. From the basic shape, molded from snow, the character of each snowman is influenced by the imagination of the creator and the decorative materials that are available.

MATERIALS AND TOOLS

3 plastic-foam balls—about 3½, 5, and 6½ inches in diameter
White glue—clear-drying
Toothpicks
Small twigs
Ruler
Paper toweling
Metylan Art Paste (or other mâché paste)
Paintbrush
Gesso
Acrylic paints—white, orange, black
Tiny stones for eyes, mouth, buttons
Krylon Spray Fixative® (or other permanent protective coating)
Discarded stretch sock for stocking cap
Yarn for pom-pom
Needle
Thread
Straw for broom
Felt or fabric scrap for scarf
Nylon fishing line for hanging

HOW TO MAKE

1. Connect the 3 plastic-foam balls of "snow" with glue-covered toothpicks inserted between each ball (fig. 1).

2. Insert a small twig into each side of the middle ball for arms.

3. Cover the balls with ¾ x 2-inch torn paper-towel strips that have been dipped in mâché paste. Cover the snowman completely, overlapping the strips. Apply at least 2 layers of strips. Model a carrot-shaped nose from paste-covered toweling and stick to the center of the face. Let dry.

4. Apply a coat of gesso. Let dry.

5. Using acrylic paints, paint the balls white and the "carrot" nose orange.

6. Paint 10 tiny stones black for the eyes, mouth, and buttons. Let dry before gluing them to the snowman.

7. Spray with a permanent protective coating.

8. To make a stocking cap, cut off the toe section of a discarded stretch sock. Turn up the cut edge for a brim and sew a yarn pom-pom to the top of the cap (fig. 2).

9. Make a broom from a twig with lengths of straw tied to one end. Secure the twig to one of the arms with glue.

10. Make a scarf from felt or fabric scrap to tie around the snowman's neck.

11. Thread a length of nylon fishing line through the top of the stocking cap and tie to make a loop for hanging.

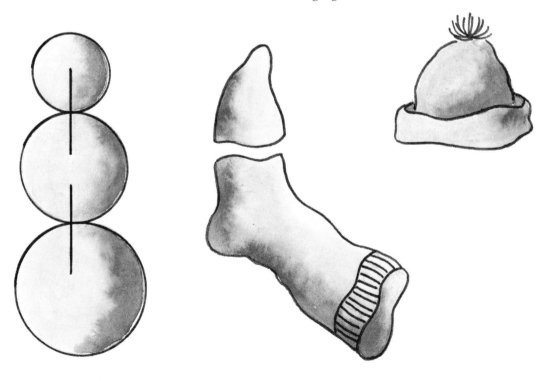

FIG.1   FIG.2

CHRISTMAS DOLLS

These festive, delightful dolls would be a welcome addition to any Christmas tree.

MATERIALS AND TOOLS

Lightweight (shirt) cardboard
Pencil
Scissors
White glue—clear-drying
Paper toweling
Florist's wire—22 gauge to make loop for hanging
Activa® Products, Inc. Celluclay
Waxed paper
Paintbrush
Gesso
Acrylic paints—assorted colors
Fabric scraps—solids and small-patterned
Ruler
Fabric trims—narrow lace, rickrack, or other trim
Needle
Thread
Yarn—lightweight, for hair
Toothpick
Acrylic polymer medium
Krylon Spray Fixative® (or other permanent protective coating)

HOW TO MAKE

1. Enlarge and trace the pattern on lightweight (shirt) cardboard (fig. 1). Cut out.

2. To make the body, roll the cardboard into a cone, leaving about a 1-inch opening at the top. Secure with glue (fig. 2).

3. To make a head and neck, wad a sheet of paper toweling into a ball about the size of a cotton ball, leaving some of the toweling at the end of the ball for a neck (fig. 3). Dampen the toweling slightly with water to help keep it together and in place.

4. Sticking the neck down inside the body, glue the head to the top of the body (fig. 4).

5. Insert a loop of fine florist's wire into the top of the head for hanging the doll once it is completed.

6. Cover the entire body and head with a thin, smooth layer of Celluclay. Keep your fingers moistened with water for easier smoothing. Work on a sheet of waxed paper so that your work can be picked up easily and moved to a drying place. Let dry.

7. Using Celluclay, mold a sleeve, arm, and hand in 1 piece on a separate sheet of waxed paper (fig. 5). Mold an arm for each side of the body. Let dry. You can hasten the drying time by placing the body and arms in an oven preheated to 150°–350° F.

8. Glue the arms to the body. Let dry.

9. Apply gesso over the entire figure. Let dry.

10. Use acrylic paints to paint a simple, easy face on the doll, such as dots for eyes, circles for cheeks, and a small heart for a mouth. Paint the body to look like it is clothed in a dress. Use a color that will complement the fabric you will be adding later for an apron.

11. Cut 1 x 2-inch piece of fabric for the bib of the apron. Fold it in half lengthwise (fig. 6). Glue it to the upper part of the dress, with the fold at the top. Cut it to size if necessary. Glue a long enough piece of narrow lace, rickrack, or other fabric trim to each side of the bib to extend over the shoulders and down to the center of the back.

12. Cut another strip of the same fabric about 2¼ x 8 inches to make the bottom half of the apron. Turn under about ¼ inch on one long side and hem (fig. 7). Add lace or other trim to the hem.

13. With needle and thread, gather the top edge of the apron with a running stitch and fit the gathered apron around the waist, covering the raw edges at the bottom of the bib. Glue in place at the wrist (fig. 8).

14. Cut short pieces of yarn for hair at the front of the head and longer lengths for hair in the back. Glue the yarn pieces to the head and "comb" it with a toothpick to make the hair style you want. Unravel some of the yarn pieces for a smoother look.

15. Glue on hair ribbons, kerchiefs, or bonnets to the head. A ribbon can be wrapped around the doll's waist and tied into a pretty bow in the back.

16. For a bonnet, use the cardboard bonnet pattern to trace around on a piece of fabric (fig. 9). Cut out and turn under all the edges ¼ inch, and then gather along the straight edge. Add a lace trim to make the bonnet stand out around the face.

17. Brush the entire doll, including the fabric, with acrylic polymer medium. This will stiffen the material. Let dry.

18. Spray the doll with a permanent protective coating.

19. To give your doll a festive holiday touch, have her holding something associated with Christmas. A tiny tray can be made with a piece of balsa wood and toothpicks and laden with Christmas cookies made from oven-baked clay. Or you can make a Christmas stocking from felt or a tiny candle and holder from a toothpick glued to a tiny button.

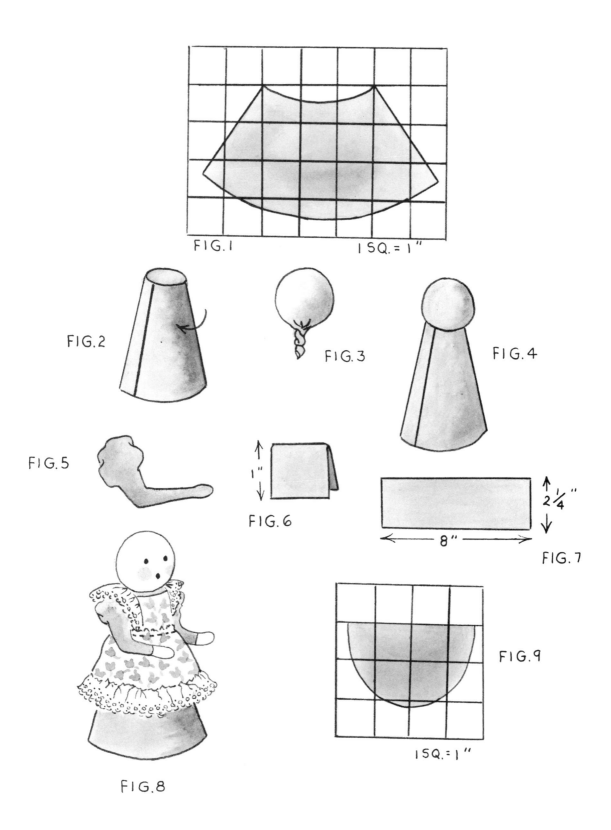

FIG.1   1 SQ. = 1"

FIG.2

FIG.3

FIG.4

FIG.5

FIG.6   1"

FIG.7   2¼"   8"

FIG.8

FIG.9   1 SQ. = 1"

"GINGERBREAD MAN" WREATH

MATERIALS AND TOOLS

Plastic-foam ring or block
White glue—clear-drying
Excelsior
Raffia—natural-colored
Westwood® Ovencraft Clay
Paintbrush
Acrylic paints
Ribbon—¾-inch wide

HOW TO MAKE

1. Purchase a white, plastic-foam ring with an approximate diameter of 3½ inches, or cut a ring from a plastic-foam block.

2. Coat both sides of the ring with glue, then press excelsior onto the glue. Let dry.

3. Wrap a length of raffia around the ring to reinforce the hold of the excelsior to the ring (fig. 1).

4. Make 3 tiny gingerbread men and 4 tiny candy canes, each about 1 inch high, from Ovencraft Clay (fig. 2). Let dry.

5. When the figures are completely dry, place them in a cold oven and bring the temperature up to 350° F. Average baking time is 1 hour.

6. Use acrylic paints to paint the figures. Allow to dry before gluing them in place around the wreath.

7. Attach a ribbon bow to the wreath and a raffia loop for hanging.

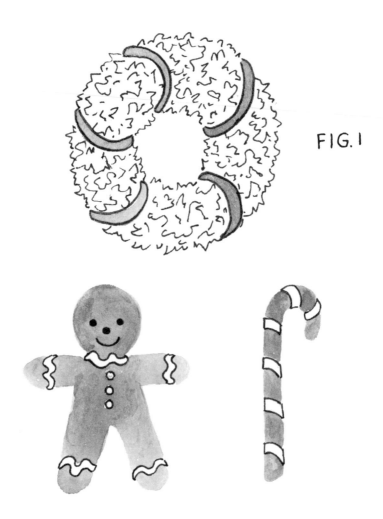

FIG. 1

FIG. 2

Everyday Early American life inspired these Weathervane ornaments, stuffed "Homespun" Barnyard Animals, Wood Shaving Chain, and ornament-sized Sioux Indian Rag Doll.

In Mexico, where they are a popular souvenir, these charming clay animals in simple shapes are often found painted in bright, festive colors.

Fabric scraps go a long way with Christmas ornaments: here, the same fabrics from which the Christmas Doll's dresses are made are also used in the stuffed Yo-Yo Wreath.

Quilling can be done with either fine wood shavings or stiff paper. These lacy Christmas designs are made by rolling and creasing narrow strips of paper into coils and scrolls.

Wood shavings make lovely, delicate ornaments such as these from Denmark: Ball, Heart, Bird, Star, and Elf.

All of these ornaments are from Central and Eastern Europe: Czechoslovakian icing Snowflakes and painted Wooden Heart; Polish Porcupine Ball, Angel, Straw Doll, and Egg Pitcher; bright German Toadstool; Austrian wood Bird.

Pantin, a simple toy with moveable joints, is painted like a French clown, with a traditional tear on his face.

Spangles, sequins, and other glittering trims decorate these felt figures, ornament adaptations of Indian shishadur embroidery.

Corn husks can be fashioned into small ornaments of remarkable variety. Simple dolls, a Basket, a Hat, and a Rose made from corn husks are complemented by a Popcorn Chain, Patchwork Star, and Mountain Wheel Star (shown in wood shavings but also possible in corn husks).

Many ornaments with a country flavor are based on everyday objects. Shown are a Berry Basket, Scarecrow, Stocking, Watermelon Slice, and the familiar Prairie Bonnet (or Sunbonnet).

Corn husk dolls take on distinct personalities when given props like Hats, Umbrellas, Flower Baskets, and Brooms. The patchwork ornaments are calico Yo-Yo Trees and Triangle Trees.

A family of Jul Nisse — Danish Christmas elves — makes a lively addition to any collection of Christmas decorations.

Traditional "tin" Mexican Christmas ornaments are painted with bright, transparent paints in colors like turquoise and magenta.

An oval shape is cut from a hollowed egg and a tiny diorama arranged within for Dutch Hollow Egg Ornaments.

China and Japan have rich folk art traditions, which supply the inspiration for these colorful ornaments: a Dragon, Fan, Hatiman Doll, Daruma Doll, Origami Peacock, Koniboro Carp, and Beckoning Cat.

The soft-sculpture "witch" is an ornament version of the benevolent witch that embodies Italian and Russian Christmas legends resembling those connected with our St. Nicholas, Santa Claus.

Mexican clay figures painted in subtle earth tones are shown with a decorative Charro Hat: neither is associated particularly with Christmas, yet they are festive and suit the bell and tiny Christmas poinsettia—which is native to Mexico and South America.

A Paper Chain appears here with some Victorian Clothespin Dolls, a Sled, and a tiny Drum that doubles as a candy container. The tall St. Nicholas container accommodates candy canes and other larger candies.

Simple felt ornaments in traditional Amish colors and patchwork block patterns draw on American folk art.

Victorian Christmas trees often had small containers holding candy or fruit. A traditional English "Cracker" can be adapted for this purpose and hung along with Band Box, Cornucopia, Gilded Egg Cup, Gilded English Walnuts, and even a tiny lady's Shoe. The Paper Rose, Heart Pincushion, and "Ribbon Candy" were all familiar to Victorians.

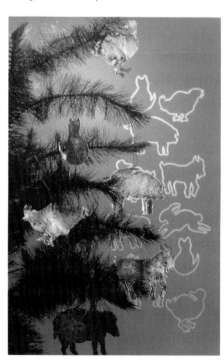

Cotton batting, glitter, and greeting-card pictures can be combined easily to make Victorian Snow Fairy and St. Nicholas figures.

"Tin" ornaments made from stiff aluminum foil are adapted from the templates used to cut animal shapes from fabric for appliqué quilts.

Victorian Tree

By the latter part of the nineteenth century, it was possible to have a lavish, ornate Christmas tree, due to the availability of store-bought ornaments. Small wooden toys, glass beads, and ball- and figure-shaped ornaments were imported from Germany. Other trimmings also became popular, such as tinsel and embossed cardboard ornaments.

Many old-fashioned Christmas tree embellishments are now being reproduced and can be purchased. These can be combined with your own elegant homemade ornaments. Garnish your ornaments with gold braids, fringes, tassels, ribbons, seed pearls, beads, and "antique" buttons; use fabrics such as lace, brocade, velvet, satin, silk, and taffeta. Effective colors to use are regal crimsons, purples, golds, and deep greens, or, for a more romantic look, pinks, lavenders, and other soft pastels.

Place small gifts such as dolls, soldiers, tops, miniature chairs, etc., on the tree branches, as they did in this era of flamboyant, opulent, tinseled elegance.

CLOTHESPIN DOLLS

The Shakers, members of a religious sect who settled in America around 1787, were the inventors of the clothespin. In the late 1800's someone discovered that the plain, ordinary clothespin could be transformed into a unique doll.

MATERIALS AND TOOLS

Wooden beads—⅝-inch for heads
Wooden clothespins with round heads
White glue—clear-drying
Paintbrush
Acrylic paints—assorted colors
Pipe cleaners—white or pink for arms
Embroidery floss
Paper for patterns
Pencil
Ruler
Scissors
Straight pins
Fabric scraps—white, assorted colors
Needle
Thread
Fabric trims—lace, patterned braid, narrow ribbon
Gold seal or gold foil wrapping paper for halo (optional)

Gauze wings (these can be found in hobby and craft shops)
Small beads for soldier's gloves
Gold cord
Small cork
Button—black, flat for hat
Tiny black beads for soldier's buttons

HOW TO MAKE THE BASIC CLOTHESPIN DOLL

1. Glue a ⅝-inch wooden bead to the top of a wooden clothespin for a head. Let dry.
2. Using acrylic paints, paint the head a flesh color. Let dry before painting on simple facial features.
3. Wind a pipe cleaner securely around the doll about ¼ inch down from the neck, leaving a 2-inch end on either side for arms. Glue in place. Bend the ends to make hands (fig. 1).

Angel

HOW TO MAKE

1. Follow the directions for the Basic Clothespin Doll.
2. To make the angel's hair, glue lengths of embroidery floss to the head. Let dry. Divide the lengths into 3 groups and braid. Wind the braid into a bun and glue in place on top of the head.
3. Trace the blouse shape onto paper to make a pattern. Cut out and pin the paper pattern to a piece of folded, white, cotton fabric. Cut out to make a front and a back (fig. 2).
4. Cut an opening for the head and a slit up the back of the blouse (fig. 3).
5. Turn the blouse inside out and stitch the sides and arm seams. Turn right-side-out. Sew a band of lace trim around the neck and around the edge of each sleeve. Put the blouse onto the angel; turn the raw edges going up the back of the blouse under, and sew together.

6. To make the skirt, cut out a 4 x 7-inch piece from the same fabric as the blouse. Hem one of the long, raw edges; then stitch a band of lace trim to the bottom of the skirt. Fold the fabric in half with the right sides facing. Stitch the short sides together, making a tube. Turn the skirt right-side-out. Turn under the other long, raw edge and baste. Slip the skirt onto the angel and pull the basting thread to gather the skirt around the waist. Using tiny stitches, sew the skirt to the blouse.
7. Wrap a narrow length of ribbon around the waist and tie in a bow.
8. Stitch a pair of wings to the back of the angel.
9. Glue a round seal (or 2 circles cut from gold foil wrapping paper and glued together gold-side-out) to the back of the head for a halo.
10. Sew a loop of gold cord or thread to the back of the angel for hanging.

Peasant Girl

HOW TO MAKE

1. Follow the directions for the Basic Clothespin Doll.

2. To make the hair, glue lengths of embroidery floss to the head. Let dry, then divide the hair on either side of the head into 3 groups and make 2 long braids. Tie bows at the ends of the braids, using embroidery floss.

3. To make the top of the dress, cut two 3-inch lengths of 1-inch-wide patterned braid. Lay 1 strip across the doll's back, covering the outstretched arms. Lay the other strip across the front. Stitch together along the shoulders, under the arms, and down the sides.

4. To make the skirt, cut a piece of fabric 3¾ x 10 inches. Stitch a narrow hem along one long edge then fold the fabric in half, right sides facing, and stitch the short sides together to make a tube. Turn right-side-out. Turn under the remaining raw edge and baste. Pull the basting thread to gather the skirt and sew it to the blouse.

5. Sew a loop of gold cord or thread to the back of the doll for hanging.

Soldier

HOW TO MAKE

1. Follow the directions for the Basic Clothespin Doll.

2. Using acrylic paints, paint on hair, blue pants, and black shoes. Paint two small beads white, for gloves. When dry, glue the beads to the ends of the pipe cleaner arms.

3. Enlarge and trace the jacket shape onto paper to make a pattern (fig. 4). Cut out. Pin the paper pattern on a folded piece of red felt, making a front and back. Cut out. Place the jacket on the soldier. Stitch or glue along the sides and under the arms to hold in place.

4. Cut out and glue a black, felt belt around the soldier's waist. Glue gold cord on the belt for a buckle and gold cord trim around the neck and sleeves of the jacket. Cut out and glue a narrow strip of white felt over each shoulder, crisscrossing in front and back. Glue tiny black beads for buttons to the right and left of the crisscross on the front, two on each side.

5. To make a hat, paint a small cork blue. Let it dry; then glue it to a black, flat button. Trim the hat with gold cord or any other trim you may have.

6. Sew a loop of gold cord or thread to the back of the soldier for hanging.

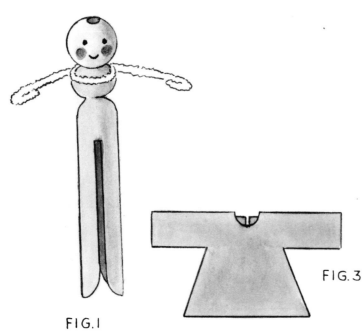

FIG.1

FIG.3

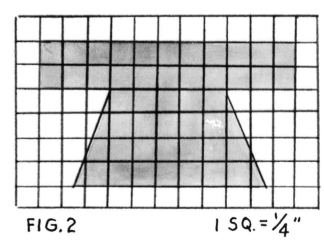

FIG.2   1 SQ. = ¼"

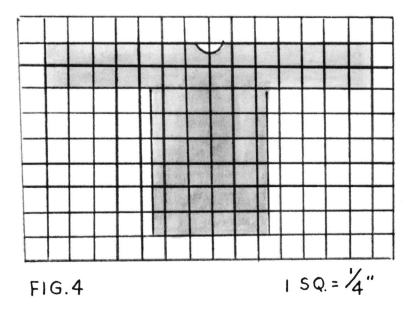

FIG. 4   1 SQ. = $\frac{1}{4}$"

PAPER CHAIN

Paper was very scarce and expensive in early America, so every piece was saved and hoarded and used only for special occasions—such as Christmas, when paper ornaments were made for the tree. Until the beginning of the nineteenth century, all paper was made by hand. The development of machine-made paper brought an increase in its use.

MATERIALS AND TOOLS

Red construction paper
Pencil
Ruler
Scissors
White glue—clear-drying

HOW TO MAKE

1. Cut several strips of red construction paper, each measuring $\frac{3}{4}$ x 6 inches.
2. Bend one of the strips into a circle, slightly overlapping the ends, and glue to secure. Loop another strip through the first circle and glue its ends. Continue in this fashion, adding strips until a desired length of chain is made. Drape the chain over the branches of the tree.

SLED

MATERIALS AND TOOLS

Popsicle sticks or craft sticks—$4\frac{1}{2}$ inches long
Ruler
Pencil
Craft knife
White glue—clear-drying
Paintbrush
Acrylic paint—red
Yarn or cord for hanging

HOW TO MAKE

1. To make the underside of the sled, cut 2 popsicle sticks as shown (fig. 1). Place the sticks on either side of two $4\frac{1}{2}$-inch sticks (fig. 2).
2. Cut 1 stick into 3 equal parts, each $1\frac{1}{2}$ inches long, to use for braces and glue to the underside of the sled (fig. 3).
3. Cut 2 sticks as shown to make runners (fig. 4).
4. Glue short edge of each runner to braces (fig. 5).

5. Cut a stick as shown for the steerer (fig. 6).

6. Turn the sled, top-side-up, and glue the steerer to the sled (fig. 7).

7. Paint the sled red.

8. Make a hole through each end of the steerer to tie a "rope" of yarn or cord for hanging.

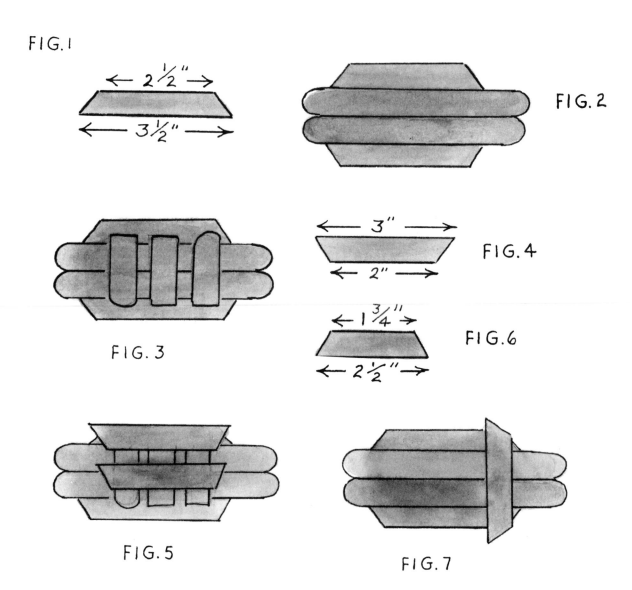

CANDY AND GIFT CONTAINERS

Christmas trees of the Victorian era were often decorated with a variety of candy and gift containers such as egg cups, gilded walnuts, and cornucopias. Also, a number of candy and gift containers were disguised as miniature cardboard replicas of drums, shoes, and bandboxes.

Bandbox

As early as the seventeenth century, bandboxes were used by American men and women for travel and storage as a catchall for hats, collarbands, and most anything else. They were made in all sizes and shapes but were usually twelve to fourteen inches tall and were made from lightweight wood or pasteboard in round or oval shapes. French wallpapers, decorated gilt and colored sheets from the Orient, and block-printed papers imported from England decorated the bandboxes. These papers were illustrated with a wide variety of scenes and designs—for example, patriotic motifs, unusual and familiar animals, historic and contemporary sites, scenes commemorating events, repeated patterns, and different modes of transportation (such as sailing ships, locomotive engines, stagecoaches, and steamboats).

MATERIALS AND TOOLS

Cardboard tube from paper toweling, waxed paper, or gift-wrap paper
Pencil
Ruler
Knife
Lightweight cardboard
Scissors
Masking tape
Wallpaper or gift-wrap paper
White glue—clear-drying
Paper clip
Decal or small, colored picture cut from a magazine, greeting card, or calendar
Narrow ribbon
Nylon fishing line for hanging

HOW TO MAKE

1. Cut a 1¾-inch section from a cardboard tube with a sharp knife (fig. 1). This will be the "body" of the box.
2. To make a bottom for the box, trace around the end of the 1¾-inch-long tube on a piece of lightweight cardboard. Cut out the cardboard circle with scissors.
3. Use strips of masking tape to fasten the bottom to the tube (figs. 2 and 3).

4. To make a lid for the box, trace around the upper end of the tube on a piece of lightweight cardboard. Then add a penciled ¼-inch border around the traced circle (fig. 4). Cut out.
5. To make a rim for the lid, use scissors to cut notches in the ¼-inch border; then turn down the resulting tabs (figs. 5 and 6).
6. To complete the rim, cut a strip of cardboard ¼ inch wide and long enough to go around and cover the tabs. Cover this cardboard strip with a ½-inch-wide strip of patterned wallpaper or gift-wrap paper, leaving a ⅛-inch overlap on each edge (fig. 7). Glue the overlap to the underside of the cardboard strip.
7. Glue the wallpaper-covered strip over the cardboard tabs on the lid. Hold in place with a paper clip until dry.
8. Cut a circle from the wallpaper to fit the top of the lid; glue in place.
9. Cut a 1¾-inch-wide wallpaper strip long enough to go around and cover the box with a slight overlap; glue in place.
10. Cut a small picture from a magazine, greeting card, or calendar, appropriate for an 18th-century bandbox, and glue it to the front of the bandbox.
11. Glue the center of a length of narrow ribbon to the bottom of the bandbox and tie it in a bow at the top of the box.
12. Glue a length of nylon fishing line to the sides of the bandbox for hanging.

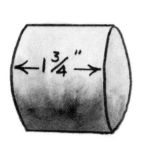

FIG. 1

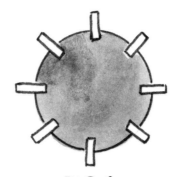

FIG. 2

FIG. 3

FIG. 4

FIG. 5

FIG. 6

CARDBOARD

FIG. 7

Drum

The drum is man's oldest instrument. Throughout history it has had many uses—it has called men to battle, been a center of ceremonial dances and religious ceremonies, served as a means of communication, and kept rhythm for military and other marching bands. It has also been a favorite Christmas toy for generations.

MATERIALS AND TOOLS

Ruler
Knife
Pencil
Cardboard mailing tube—about 3 inches in diameter
Compass
Lightweight cardboard
Scissors
White glue—clear-drying
Paintbrush
Acrylic paints—white, gold, red, blue
Small patriotic decal or picture cut from magazine, calendar, or greeting card
Darning needle for punching holes
Metallic gold cord

HOW TO MAKE

1. Cut a 2½-inch length from a cardboard tube with a sharp knife (fig. 1). This will be the "body" of the drum.

2. To make a bottom for the drum, use a compass to draw a circle slightly smaller than the circumference of the tube on a piece of lightweight cardboard. Add a penciled ¼-inch border around the drawn circle (fig. 2).

3. Using scissors, cut notches in the ¼-inch border; turn down the resulting tabs (figs. 3 and 4).

4. Place glue on the outside of the tabs and insert the tabs inside the cardboard tube, far enough in to leave a narrow rim around the bottom of the drum (figs. 5 and 6).

5. To make the top (lid) of the drum, use the compass to draw a circle slightly smaller than the circumference of the tube on a piece of lightweight cardboard. Add a penciled tab and hinge before cutting out (fig. 7).

6. Bend the tab up so that it can be used later to lift the lid. Bend the hinge down so that when the lid is closed it will not be seen (fig. 8).

7. Place glue on the hinge and insert the top (lid) into the other end of the tube far enough to leave a narrow rim around the top of the drum (fig. 9).

8. Paint the drum with acrylic paints—the bottom and top of the drum white and the rest of the drum in patriotic colors of red, blue, and gold. Let dry.

9. Glue a small patriotic decal or a colored picture cut from a magazine, calendar, or greeting card to the drum.

10. For lacing, punch holes around the bottom and top rims using a darning needle, alternating the spacing (fig. 10).

11. Lace the drum with gold metallic cord going from a hole in the top rim to a hole in the bottom rim, then back to another hole in the top rim, etc., going around the entire drum.

12. Attach a looped piece of gold cord for hanging.

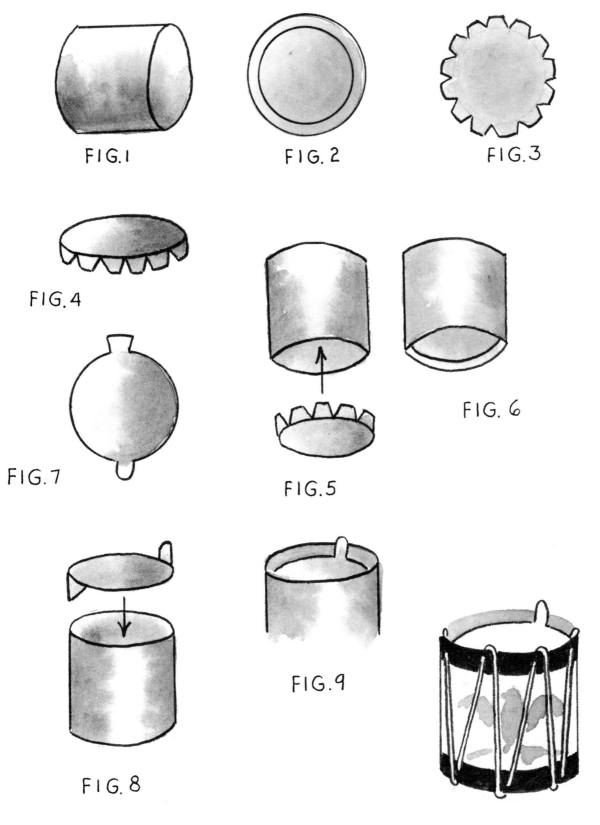

FIG.1

FIG.2

FIG.3

FIG.4

FIG.5

FIG. 6

FIG.7

FIG. 8

FIG.9

FIG.10

Shoe

MATERIALS AND TOOLS

Aluminum foil
Ruler
Scissors
Waxed paper
Activa Products® Celluclay
Paintbrush
Gesso
Acrylic paints—black or brown and color to match
  fabric
Lightweight cardboard
White glue—clear-drying
Fabric—6 x 10 inches
Narrow lace or other fancy trim
Narrow ribbon
Elegant small button, bead, or piece of old costume
  jewelry
Nylon fishing line for hanging
Krylon Spray Fixative® (or other permanent protective
  coating)

HOW TO MAKE

1. Start at one end of a 12 x 30-inch piece of aluminum foil and begin to form a toe of a shoe by gently squeezing the foil. Gradually work up the shoe to the heel, shaping the foil as you go. Be sure to leave an indentation at the top of the shoe where a foot would go into a shoe. Add pieces of foil as needed or cut away any excess foil until the shoe measures approximately $2\frac{1}{2}$ inches from the top of the shoe to the bottom of the heel and 4 inches from the heel to the toe (fig. 1).

2. Working on a sheet of waxed paper, model and shape the shoe further by filling any holes in the foil with Celluclay.

3. Cover the entire shoe with a thin, smooth layer of Celluclay. Keep your finger moistened with water for easier smoothing. Let dry.

4. Apply gesso over the entire shoe. Let dry.

5. Paint the shoe with acrylic paints, using colors that coordinate with the fabric you have chosen for the bag, which will be later attached to the shoe to hold a gift or candies. Let dry.

6. To make a sole and a heel plate for the shoe, set the shoe on a piece of lightweight cardboard and trace around the sole and heel (fig. 2). Cut out; paint with black or brown acrylic paints. Let dry before gluing to the bottom of the shoe.

7. Spray the shoe with a permanent protective coating. Let dry.

8. To make the bag, cut a piece of fabric 6 x 10 inches. Sew a narrow hem in one long edge of the fabric. Stitch a row of lace or other fancy trim to the hem. This will be the top of the bag.

9. Fold the 6 x 10-inch piece of fabric in half, right sides together, and stitch the side and bottom (fig. 3). Turn right-side-out.

10. Glue the bottom of the bag into the foot opening of the shoe. Let dry.

11. Tack a length of narrow ribbon near the top of the bag; wrap it around the bag to close it and tie into a bow.

12. Glue an elegant button, bead, or piece of old jewelry to the front of the shoe.

13. Attach a loop of nylon fishing line for hanging.

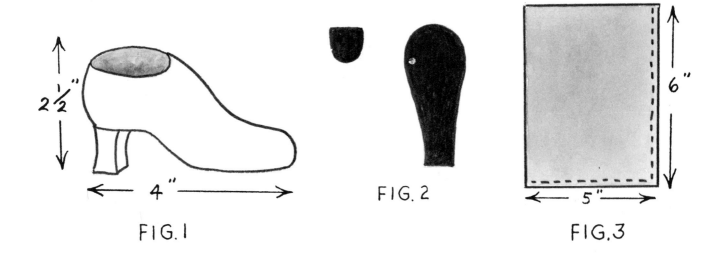

FIG.1

FIG.2

FIG.3

Gilded Egg Cup

During the Victorian period, eggs were carefully broken in the middle, gilded, then decorated with colorful embossed, die-cut pictures imported from Germany. These pictures were of Santa heads, wreaths, cherubs, hearts, roses, Christmas trees, doves, and other sentimental images. Filled with Christmas goodies, the egg cup made a dainty and delicate ornament for the tree.

MATERIALS AND TOOLS

Egg
Pencil
Transparent tape
Manicure scissors
Paintbrush
Acrylic paints
White glue—clear-drying
Decal or small picture cut from magazine, seed catalog, or gift-wrap paper
Krylon Spray Fixative® (or other permanent protective coating)
Decorative trim—lace or gold braid
Gold thread for hanging

HOW TO MAKE

1. Without removing the contents of an egg, pencil a line around the middle of it (fig. 1). This will be the cutting line. Place a strip of transparent tape over the penciled line to reinforce the shell before cutting.

2. Using the point of manicure scissors, make a small hole in the shell somewhere along the penciled line and then make 2 halves by cutting around the line.

3. Remove the tape, wash out each half of the shell, and let dry.

4. Leave the shells their natural color or tint them with acrylic paints to provide color contrast for the pictures you have chosen to decorate the egg cups. Let dry.

5. Glue small decals to the shells or substitute paper cutouts from gift-wrap, seed catalogs, or magazines. If the paper is too heavy to fit around the contour of the shells, cut tiny slashes around the pictures before gluing them to the shells.

6. Apply a coat of permanent protective fixative to the shells.

7. Glue decorative lace trim or gold braid around the top edges of the shells.

8. Glue a length of gold thread inside the egg cups, going from one side to the other, for hanging.

FIG. 1

Gilded English Walnut

MATERIALS AND TOOLS

English walnut
Knife
Gold leaf enamel
White glue—clear-drying
Gold thread or narrow velvet ribbon for hanging
Small gift

HOW TO MAKE

1. Heat the walnut in a 300° F oven for 20 minutes or until the shell can be pried open easily when the tip of a knife blade is inserted into the seam. Empty the nut of its meats.

2. Paint the inside and outside of the 2 halves of the nut with gold leaf enamel. Let dry.

3. Glue a loop of gold thread or narrow velvet ribbon inside one end of one of the half shells for hanging.

4. Place a small gift inside the shell, then seal the pair of half shells with only a few dabs of glue, so that it can be opened easily.

Santa Claus Container

Our Santa Claus of today evolved from Saint Nicholas, a bishop who lived in the Middle East around 300 A.D. According to legend, he was unusually kind and would often go out at night to give gifts to the poor. He became a favorite saint, and, after his death, his fame spread throughout Europe. For hundreds of years, people celebrated the feast of Saint Nicholas on December 6th—and still do in many European countries. The custom of celebrating Saint Nicholas Day and giving gifts was brought to America by Dutch settlers.

In America, in the early 1800's, due to illustrations and literature, the European version of the tall, thin, dignified Saint Nicholas changed to the familiar short, fat, jolly Santa Claus.

MATERIALS AND TOOLS

Cardboard tube from paper toweling, waxed paper, or gift-wrap paper
Pencil
Ruler
Knife
Construction paper—red or green
Scissors
Lightweight cardboard
Masking tape
White glue—clear-drying
Santa figure—approximately 6 inches high, cut from greeting card, gift-wrap paper, or magazine
Colored cord or thread for hanging

HOW TO MAKE

1. Cut a 4½-inch length from a cardboard tube with a sharp knife (fig. 1).

2. To make a bottom for the tube, trace around the end of the tube on a piece of lightweight cardboard. Cut out the cardboard circle with scissors.

3. Use strips of masking tape to fasten the bottom to the tube (figs. 2 and 3). This makes the container to hold the gifts or candies.

4. To decorate the cardboard container, cut a red or green circle from construction paper to fit the bottom of the tube, and a rectangular strip long enough to go around and cover the tube with a slight overlap. Glue in place.

5. Cut a Santa figure, about 6 inches in height, from a greeting card, gift-wrap paper, or magazine and glue it to a piece of lightweight cardboard.

6. Cut out the cardboard-backed Santa and glue it to the front of the cardboard tube. Let dry.

7. Punch a small hole at the top of each side of the tube and tie a length of colored cord or thread through the holes for hanging.

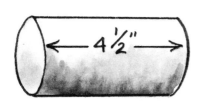

FIG.1

FIG.2

FIG.3

German Cornucopia

The cornucopia, also called the horn of plenty and used as a symbol of nature's bounty, had its origin in Greek mythology. According to a myth, Zeus, in gratitude, gave a goat's horn to the nurses who fed him goat's milk as an infant. The horn could be filled with whatever the nurses wished.

Cornucopias filled with candies, fruits, nuts, and tiny gifts have been used in Germany for many years as Christmas-tree decorations. This custom was brought to America by the German colonists.

MATERIALS AND TOOLS

Compass
Ruler
Pencil
Lightweight cardboard—12 x 12 inches
Scissors
Gift-wrap paper, wallpaper, foil, or fabric to cover cone
White glue—clear-drying
Decorative trim—ribbon, rickrack, lace, braid, or eyelet
Ribbon, yarn, or cord for hanging

HOW TO MAKE

1. Using a compass, draw a circle 12 inches in diameter on lightweight cardboard. Divide the circle into quarters, and cut out 1 quarter to use for a cornucopia. Repeat the same process using wallpaper, gift-wrap paper, foil, or fabric, and glue the decorative circle to the cardboard one to make an attractive cover.

2. Bend the covered cardboard into a cone shape, overlapping the edges. Glue the edges together and allow to dry (fig. 1).

3. Glue ribbon, lace, rickrack, braid, eyelet or other decorative trim around the rim of the cone.

4. To make a loop for hanging, glue one end of a length of yarn, ribbon, or cord inside the cone to one side, then glue the other end to the opposite side.

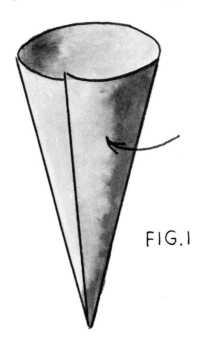

FIG.1

English Cracker

The "exploding" English cracker at the Christmas table has been a British tradition for many years. It was invented by Tom Smith in 1840 and has never lost its fascination. The early crackers were filled with miniature books, jewelry, crowns, toys, flowers, bottles of perfume, etc. By 1900 the manufacturing of crackers had become a minor industry.

The cracker made here is not designed to "pop" but rather to be used as a decorative container to hold Christmas gifts or candies.

MATERIALS AND TOOLS

Cardboard tube—5-inch length from inside paper toweling, toilet paper, or gift-wrap
Crepe or tissue paper—12 x 12 inches
Scissors
Yarn, cord, or ribbon for tying ends
White glue—clear-drying
Decorative paper seal or small decorative picture
Nylon fishing line for hanging

HOW TO MAKE

1. Wrap candies or a small gift and place inside a 5-inch-long cardboard tube.

2. Wrap the cardboard tube with a 12 x 12-inch square of crepe or tissue paper, letting it extend beyond the tube on both sides. Twist the ends of the paper and fringe with scissors. Tie, making a bow over each end with a 14-inch length of yarn, cord, or ribbon.

3. Stick a purchased decorative seal or glue a small picture cut from a magazine or greeting card on the center of the cracker where the tissue or crepe paper overlaps. You can also make a seal by gluing a colorful picture cut from a greeting card, gift-wrap paper, or magazine onto the cracker.

4. Attach nylon fishing line to one end of the cracker to make a loop for hanging.

HEART PINCUSHION

Pincushions of one kind or another have been used ever since early man needed to protect and store fragile pins made from sharp thorns or animal bones. During the Victorian period, many elaborate pincushions were made to serve no other purpose than to decorate a wall.

MATERIALS AND TOOLS

Pencil
Paper for pattern
Scissors
Straight pins
Fabric—14 inches square
Fabric trim—lace ruffling, eyelet ruffling, or piping
Needle
Thread
Polyester fiberfill
Narrow ribbon for hanging

HOW TO MAKE

1. Enlarge the heart shape to make a paper pattern (fig. 1). Cut out.

2. Pin the paper pattern to a 14-inch-square piece of folded fabric to make 2 hearts. Cut out. A seam allowance of $\frac{1}{4}$ inch is included.

3. Pin and stitch a fabric trim (such as lace ruffling, eyelet ruffling, or piping) around one of the hearts (right-side-up). Keep the fabric trim facing the center of the heart (fig. 2) and put your line of stitching just outside the $\frac{1}{4}$-inch seam allowance.

4. Pin the other heart on top of the heart with the fabric trim, keeping the right sides together and matching edges. Stitch the 2 hearts together right inside the line of stitching from the trim and leaving an opening for turning.

5. Clip curves and turn right-side-out. Stuff lightly with fiberfill and stitch the opening closed.

6. Sew a loop of narrow ribbon to the top of the heart for hanging.

SEAM ALLOWANCE INCLUDED

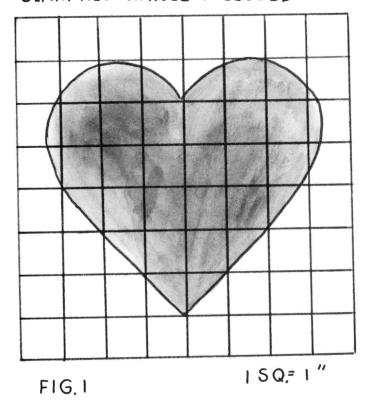

FIG. 1

I SQ. = 1"

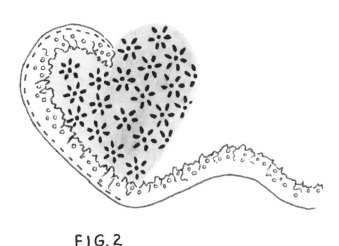

FIG. 2

PAPIER MÂCHÉ RIBBON CANDY

MATERIALS AND TOOLS

Construction paper—white, heavy
Pencil
Ruler
Scissors
Metylan Art Paste (or other mâché paste)
Waxed paper
Felt pens—permanent, fine-tipped, in a variety of colors
Krylon Spray Fixative® (or other permanent protective coating)
Nylon fishing line for hanging

HOW TO MAKE

1. For each piece of "candy," cut a 1 x 9-inch strip from heavy, white construction paper.

2. Dip the strip in mâché paste and slide it between 2 fingers to free it of any excess paste.

3. Holding one end of the strip with your fingers, place the other end on a sheet of waxed paper and begin to layer the strip by folding and reversing the direction every 1½ inches of the strip (fig. 1). Let dry.

4. Using permanent, fine-tipped felt pens, paint the folded strip with various widths of brightly colored stripes to resemble ribbon candy.

5. Spray with a permanent protective coating.

6. Thread a length of nylon fishing line through one of the folds in the "candy" to make a loop for hanging.

FIG. 1

PAPER ROSE

Paper roses of many different colors have been a favorite Christmas decoration for several centuries. The rose has been a symbol for the Virgin Mary since early Christianity. A German legend further enhances the use of the rose as a Christmas decoration. According to the legend, a heavenly radiance occurred on the night Jesus was born, causing the winter snow to melt and the roses to burst into bloom.

The rose was also a favorite decorative motif of the Victorian era. With the development of machine-made paper, and the lowering of its price, Victorian ladies took up the craft of paper flower making. Consequently, the paper rose adorned many of the Christmas trees of this romantic era.

MATERIALS AND TOOLS

Crepe paper—red, green
Pencil
Ruler
Scissors
Cellophane tape
Florist's wire—22 gauge for stem
Floral tape—green
White paper doily (5-inch diameter)
Pink ribbon—$2\frac{1}{2}$ inches long, $\frac{3}{8}$ inches wide

HOW TO MAKE

1. Cut 2 strips of red crepe paper, each $3\frac{1}{4}$ x 20 inches.
2. Fold each strip in eighths and cut as shown (figs. 1 and 2).
3. Unfold each strip, and tape the two together so they overlap (fig. 3).

4. Starting from one end, begin to roll tightly about $2\frac{1}{2}$ inches of the strip, then gather at the base. Fold a 10-inch length of florist's wire in half and twist it tightly around the base; then bring the wire ends down for a stem. Continue to roll the rest of the strip, securing the gathers at the base with cellophane tape (fig. 4).

5. To give shape to the rose, gently stretch and cup the centers of each petal to open them a little. Slightly roll down the top of each petal.

6. Cut and serrate three 2 x 4-inch leaves (fig. 5). Tape them around the base of the rose.

7. Wrap all exposed cellophane tape, petal ends, and wire stem with green floral tape.

8. Push the stem through the center of a 5-inch white paper doily and tie a ribbon bow on the stem.

9. Attach the rose to the tree by bending the stem around a tree branch.

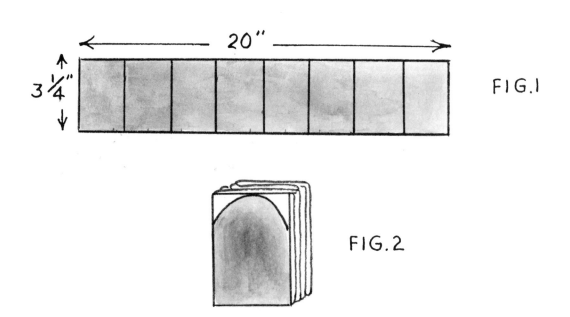

20"

$3\frac{1}{4}$"

FIG.1

FIG.2

FIG. 3

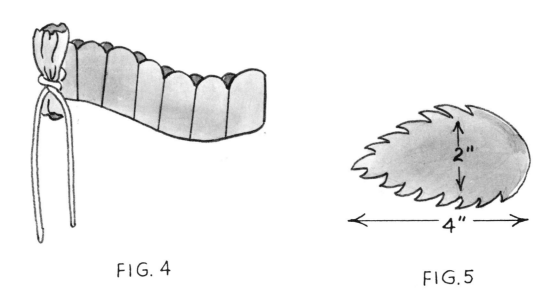

FIG. 4

FIG. 5

GERMAN LEBKUCHEN COOKIES

German lebkuchen cookies are made with a spicy, honey-fragrant gingerbread dough. They are a specialty of the German city of Nuremberg and were baked as early as the beginning of the sixteenth century. Seven spices were baked in the cookie in memory of the seven days in which God created the world.

During the Victorian period in America, these cookies were decorated with colorful, embossed Christmas motifs such as angels, Santa Clauses, the Holy Family, doves, etc., to be hung on the Christmas tree.

INGREDIENTS

$\frac{3}{4}$ cup honey
$\frac{3}{4}$ cup firmly packed, dark-brown sugar
1 egg
2 teaspoons grated lemon rind
3 tablespoons lemon juice
$3\frac{1}{2}$ cups sifted all-purpose flour
1 teaspoon salt
1 teaspoon ground cinnamon
1 teaspoon ground nutmeg
$\frac{1}{2}$ teaspoon ground allspice
$\frac{1}{2}$ teaspoon ground ginger
$\frac{1}{4}$ teaspoon ground cloves
$\frac{1}{2}$ teaspoon baking soda
8 ounces finely chopped citron
1 cup chopped unblanched almonds

MATERIALS AND TOOLS

Drinking straw
Pastry brush (for glaze)
Christmas motifs—may be cut from heavy gift-wrap or greeting cards, or paper decals
Nylon fishing line for hanging

HOW TO MAKE

1. Plan to make the dough several days in advance, or at least the night before, to allow the dough to "ripen."

2. Heat honey to boiling in a small saucepan; pour into a large bowl; cool about 30 minutes.

3. Stir in brown sugar, egg, lemon rind, and lemon juice. Blend well.

4. Sift flour, salt, cinnamon, nutmeg, allspice, ginger, cloves, and baking soda into a bowl.

5. Stir flour mixture into honey mixture a third at a time. Stir in citron and almonds. Dough will be sticky. Wrap in foil; chill several hours, or until firm.

6. Roll out dough $\frac{3}{8}$-inch thick on floured surface. Cut into squares or rectangles. Place 1 inch apart on greased cookie sheet.

7. Use a drinking straw to make a hole at the top of each cookie for hanging.

8. Bake in moderate oven 350° F for 20 minutes or until the cookies are firm and are very lightly browned. Remove to a wire rack.

9. While cookies are hot, brush with hot Sugar Glaze (recipe follows), then press on a paper decal or a picture cut from heavy gift-wrap paper or greeting card. Store the cooled cookies in a tightly covered container in a cool, dry place at least 2 weeks, to mellow.

10. Thread a length of nylon fishing line through the hole and tie the ends to make a loop for hanging.

SUGAR GLAZE

Combine $1\frac{1}{2}$ cups granulated sugar and $\frac{3}{4}$ cup water in a medium-size saucepan and bring to boiling. Reduce heat and simmer 3 minutes. Remove from heat; stir in $\frac{1}{2}$ cup sifted, confectioners (powdered) sugar. Makes about 2 cups.

Yield: 5 dozen $2\frac{1}{2}$ x $1\frac{1}{2}$-inch cookies

PAPER QUILLED ORNAMENTS

Paper quilling is the art of rolling, bending, and creasing narrow strips of paper into coils and scrolls, then joining them with glue into decorative, lacy designs. Originally the coils were formed around feather quills, thus the name "quilling."

Quilling dates back at least to the fifteenth century in Europe. It most likely began in European monasteries, where worn paper from old books and bibles were recycled into thin strips to be used for quilling. The coils and scrolls were pasted together to reproduce biblical scenes, to decorate religious plaques and paintings, to be used as backgrounds for statues, and to make frames for important documents.

Quilling was brought to America by women who settled in the colonies. They used it to decorate such things as tea caddies, frames, mirrors, boxes, and candle sconces. It became a fashionable hobby during the Victorian period, when ladies were eager for a new vogue to replace the embroidery crafts. Also, it involved little expense, was a simple method to master, and appealed to the Victorian fondness for laciness.

MATERIALS AND TOOLS

Construction paper in assorted colors, or any paper
   thin enough to curl and sturdy enough to hold its
   shape
Pencil
Ruler
Scissors
Paper cutter (optional)
Corrugated cardboard
Waxed paper
Toothpick
White glue—clear-drying
Straight pins
Tweezers
Krylon Spray Fixative® (or other permanent protective
   coating)

HOW TO MAKE

1. Choose a design that you wish to make. There are endless possibilities—angels, Christmas trees, snowflakes, flowers, hearts, bells, snowmen, wreaths, and so forth (some of which are shown on page 52).

2. Measure, then cut $\frac{1}{8}$-inch-wide strips, 2 to 6 inches long, from thin construction paper of various colors.

3. Prepare a working surface with a piece of corrugated cardboard covered with waxed paper.

4. Dampen the end of each strip before rolling it around a toothpick. Roll tightly, keeping the edges even.

5. Carefully remove the rolled strip from the toothpick. Keep it tight or loose depending on the type of roll or scroll shape you need to build the design. See the Basic Rolls and Scrolls (fig. 1). Glue down the outside end to keep the roll from completely unwinding.

6. Using a straight pin, secure the roll or scroll to the cardboard working surface. Continue to build your design by gluing each finished roll to a previously made roll (fig. 2). It is easier to start from the center with most designs. Tweezers help to lift and set the paper shapes in place.

7. Spray the finished design with a permanent protective coating.

8. Remove the straight pins and lift the ornament from the waxed paper. Attach to the tree with an ornament hanger.

BASIC ROLLS

FIG. 1

loose roll

heart

triangle

eye

raindrop

square

tight roll

SCROLLS

scroll

"S" shape

"V" shape

heart

decorative scroll

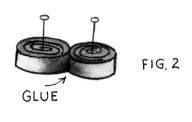

GLUE

FIG. 2

FRENCH PANTIN

This simple, amusing toy dates back to the sixteenth century. It is made of wood, cardboard, or other materials and is manipulated by means of a thread. In France it's called Pantin. In Germany it's called Hampelmann. In England and the United States, it's called Jumping Jack.

During the nineteenth century, German toymakers exported a number of these gaily painted, jointed soldiers, Santas, princesses, harlequins, etc., to America. You can be reasonably sure that many of these found their way to the Christmas tree.

MATERIALS AND TOOLS

Pencil
Ruler
Scissors
Stiff cardboard that can be cut with scissors
Paper hole-punch
Felt pens—fine-tipped, black, light blue, pink
½-inch brass fasteners
Needle with large eye
Heavy string
Small wooden bead (optional)
Paintbrush
Acrylic paints—black, white
Nylon fishing line for hanging

HOW TO MAKE

1. To make "Pierrot," the French clown, enlarge and transfer patterns to stiff cardboard (fig. 1). Cut out.

2. Use a paper hole-punch to make holes in the body parts where they will join. Punch holes where indicated on the patterns.

3. Color Pierrot's facial features and his black and white costume using fine-tipped felt pens. Don't forget to paint a blue tear drop on his face (fig. 2).

4. Fasten the arms and legs loosely with brass fasteners. Leave a little space between the parts when you open the prongs of the fastener so that the parts can move more easily.

5. Working on the back side of the figure, join the arms by running a needle threaded with a 4-inch length of string through the holes. Tie in a knot. Connect the legs in the same way (fig. 3).

6. Tie a third 12-inch length of string, connecting the arm and leg strings (fig. 4). Pull this string to make the clown jump. You may want to tie a small wooden bead to the end of this string to make pulling easier.

7. Paint the heads of the brass fasteners with acrylic paint to make them less conspicuous.

8. Thread a length of nylon fishing line through the top of Pierrot's hat and tie to make a loop for hanging.

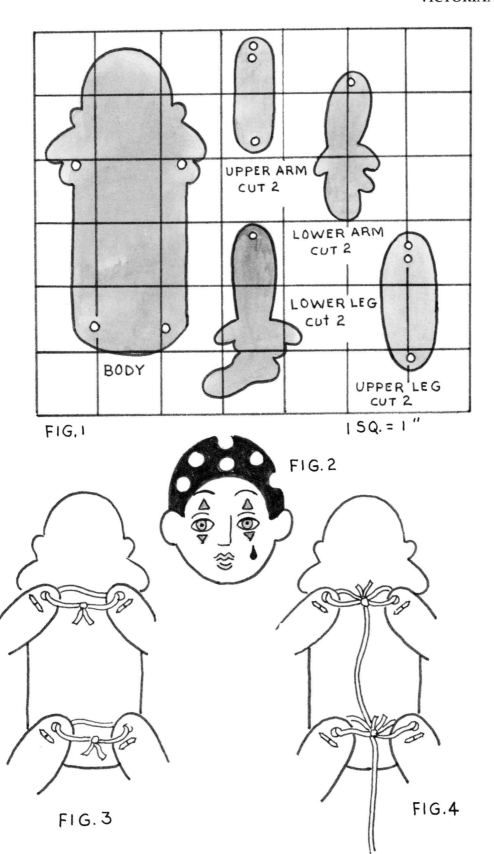

FIG. 1

UPPER ARM
CUT 2

LOWER ARM
CUT 2

LOWER LEG
CUT 2

UPPER LEG
CUT 2

BODY

1 SQ. = 1"

FIG. 2

FIG. 3

FIG. 4

SNOW FAIRY AND SAINT NICHOLAS

During the latter part of the nineteenth century, Christmas ornaments from the German cottage industry were imported to the United States. Families in Germany made figures of Saint Nicholas and Snow Fairies cut from cardboard with glued-on, glossy, embossed printed faces. The figures were clothed with thin cotton batting sprinkled with glistening glass particles, to look like fallen snow.

MATERIALS AND TOOLS

Lightweight cardboard
Scissors
Pencil
Santa and angel faces cut from greeting cards, or purchased stickers

White glue—clear-drying
Cotton batting—thin
Seed beads for buttons
Silver glitter
Twigs for Santa to hold
Nylon fishing line for hanging

Snow Fairy

HOW TO MAKE

1. Cut a background shape from lightweight cardboard. This shape should follow the contour of a fairy wearing a bonnet and a coat and must correspond in size to the face you are planning to use (figs. 1—2).
2. Glue the face in place on the cardboard.
3. Cut 2 bonnet and 2 coat shapes from cotton batting and glue in place on the front and back sides of the cardboard.

4. Glue additional cotton batting shapes to the fairy to make a cape or a muff. Tiny seed beads can be glued on for buttons.
5. Glue glitter in places on the batting to look like fallen snow.
6. Thread a length of nylon fishing line through the top of the bonnet and tie to make a loop for hanging.

Saint Nicholas

In Germany, Saint Nicholas checks each child's behavior. He leaves little presents as a reward for the good children, but the naughty ones receive a bundle of rods as a warning.

HOW TO MAKE

1. Cut a lightweight cardboard backing following the contour of Saint Nicholas wearing a tall hat and a long coat (fig. 3). Keep the size of the cardboard shape in relation to the size of the face you are planning to use.
2. Glue a Santa face in place on the cardboard.
3. Cut 2 hat shapes and 2 coat shapes from cotton batting and glue in place to the front and back sides of the cardboard.

4. Glue a bundle of small twigs to one side of the coat.
5. Cut 2 pieces of cotton batting in the shape of sleeves and glue to the front of the cotton batting coat, gluing one sleeve over the twigs. Add a cotton batting collar, sleeve cuffs, and hat brim.
6. Glue silver glitter in places on the hat and coat to look like snow.
7. Thread a length of nylon fishing line through the top of the hat and tie to make a loop for hanging.

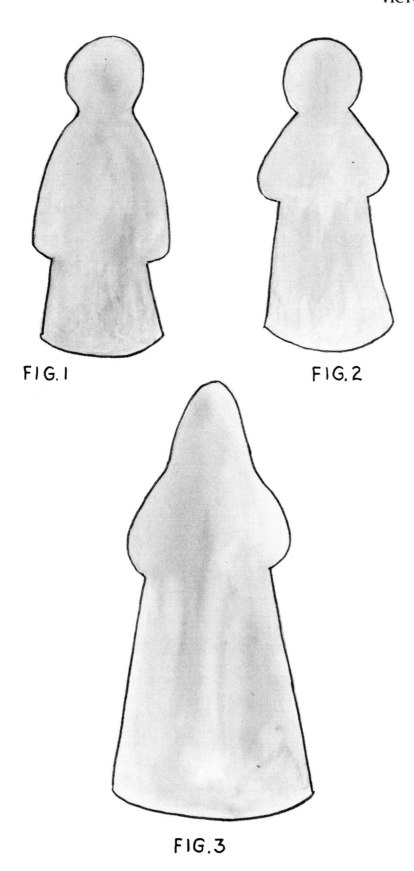

FIG. 1

FIG. 2

FIG. 3

International Tree

An international tree can be decorated with a rich and varied blend of ornaments representing several different countries. Every nationality has some unique ornaments. People from the Northern, Central, and Eastern European countries traditionally use farm materials such as eggs, feathers, nuts, and straw for their Christmas ornaments. Scandinavian tree ornaments are usually made from wood, grain, and greenery using red, blue, white, gold, and natural wood or straw colors. The Oriental's expert stylization and simplicity and the Latin American's love of vivid and gay colors add a new and distinctive flavor to our Christmas heritage.

Let your tree foster friendship and world peace.

AUSTRIA

Bird

MATERIALS AND TOOLS

Paper for pattern
Pencil
Ruler
Scissors
$\frac{1}{8}$-inch-thick plywood—4 x 5 inches
Jigsaw or coping saw
Sandpaper
Paintbrush
Gesso
Acrylic paints—red, blue, yellow
Drill with $\frac{1}{8}$-inch drill bit
Soft wood, such as pine—$\frac{3}{4}$ x 14 inches
Vise
Wood plane
White glue—clear-drying
Bobby pins
Nylon fishing line for hanging

HOW TO MAKE

1. Enlarge and trace around the bird shape to make a paper pattern (fig. 1). Cut out.

2. Trace around the paper pattern onto plywood and cut out with a jigsaw or coping saw.

3. Smooth the edges with sandpaper.

4. Apply gesso to both sides of the wood to seal it. Let dry.

5. Paint the bird red, add a round yellow eye with a blue center and a yellow beak with acrylic paints. Let dry.

6. Drill a hole using a $\frac{1}{8}$-inch drill bit at the top of the bird for hanging. See the X on the pattern for placement of hole.

7. Soak a 14-inch length of $\frac{3}{4}$-inch pine in water at least 8 hours; then place in a vise and plane off three 14-inch-long, thin strips.

8. Bend each strip as shown for a tail and wings (figs. 2 and 3). Hold the folded strips in place with dabs of glue and bobby pins until dry.

9. Glue the wings and tail to the bird.

10. Thread a length of nylon fishing line through the hole and tie ends together to make a loop for hanging.

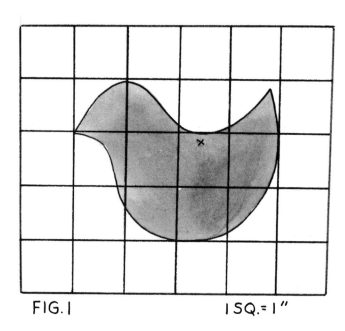

FIG.1   1 SQ.= 1"

FIG.2

FIG.3

CHINA

Dragon

The dragon is the most common and important of all Chinese artistic symbols. During the Chinese New Year, dragons with huge, bright green and gold papier mâché heads weave through the streets. The dragons have long, red capes attached, concealing people underneath who provide the dragon's support. During this celebration drums are heard banging while loud fire crackers explode, representing thunder and lightning to wake up the rain dragons.

In China dragons are considered to be good creatures, since they bring life-giving rains. Dragons in most countries, on the other hand, are regarded as being evil and destructive.

MATERIALS AND TOOLS

Aluminum foil
Pencil
Ruler
Scissors
Masking tape
Florist's wire—22 gauge to make loop for hanging
Waxed paper
Activa® Products, Inc. Celluclay
Paper toweling
Metylan Art Paste (or other mâché paste)
Paintbrush
Gesso
Acrylic paints—green, red, white, black, pink
Gold leaf enamel
Krylon Spray Fixative® (or other permanent protective coating)
Fabric—red, 7 x 9 inches
Fabric trim—metallic gold

HOW TO MAKE

1. Form a dragon's head with open jaws from a piece of 12 x 30-inch aluminum foil by gently crushing it into shape. You may find it necessary to cut the foil in places or to add foil. Hold the foil in place with masking tape. The head and neck combined should measure about 5 inches long (fig. 1).

2. Insert the twisted ends of a loop of florist's wire into the top of the head for hanging the ornament after it is completed.

3. Work on waxed paper. For ease in handling, cover just one side of the head and neck with a smooth layer of Celluclay. Moisten your finger with water for easier smoothing. Build up an ear, nostril, and a bump at the top of the head with the Celluclay. Let dry, then turn the head over and repeat the procedure (fig. 2). Let dry.

4. Cut a row of spikes to run down the back of the neck and a long tongue from 4 layers of paper toweling. Dip in mâché paste; squeeze out the excess paste and attach to the dragon (fig. 3).

5. Mold pointed teeth to the upper and lower jaw with Celluclay. Let dry.

6. Apply a coat of gesso over the entire dragon. Let dry.

7. Using acrylic paints, paint the dragon's head and neck green. Use gold leaf enamel to paint the spikes and to paint gold scales on the neck. Paint a menacing black-and-white eye, black eyebrows, white teeth, pink mouth interior, and a red tongue (fig. 4). Let dry.

8. Spray with a permanent protective coating.

9. Make a red cape from fabric, 7 x 9 inches. Hem on all sides. Sew metallic gold fabric trim to each of the long edges.

10. Glue one of the short edges of the cape to the dragon's neck.

FIG. 1

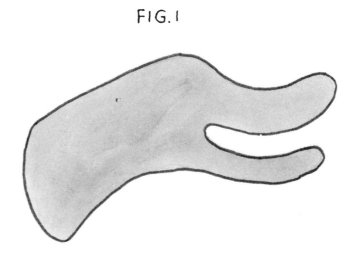

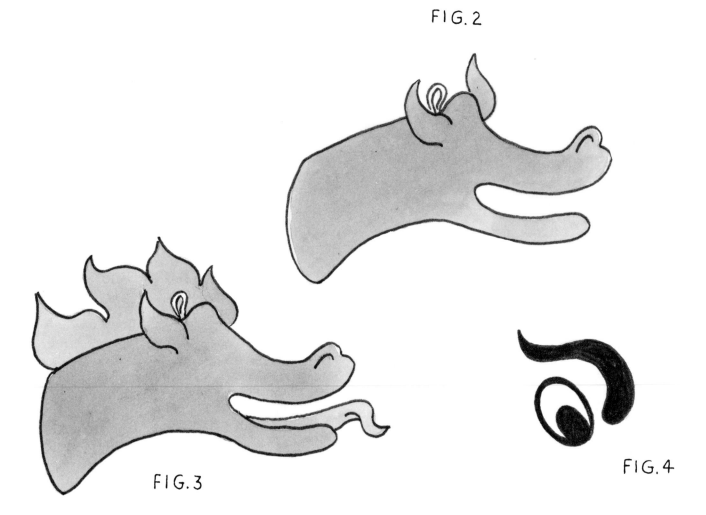

FIG. 2

FIG. 3

FIG. 4

CZECHOSLOVAKIA

Snowflake Ornaments

INGREDIENTS

1 cup powdered sugar
1 egg white
$\frac{1}{8}$ teaspoon cream of tartar
Pastry tube

HOW TO MAKE

1. Draw snowflake designs about 3 inches in diameter onto paper. Place the designs beneath a piece of waxed paper to use as a guide.

2. Beat egg white and cream of tartar until stiff, then slowly add the sugar, beating constantly until the mixture is thick.

3. Spoon frosting into a pastry tube with a medium-size writing tip. Cover the remaining frosting so that no air can get to it. Stir from time to time to prevent hardening or sugaring. This frosting will not keep overnight.

4. Pipe frosting onto the waxed paper following the lines of the designs. Allow to harden overnight.

5. Gently peel off the waxed paper and string the snowflakes with nylon fishing line for hanging.

Yield: About 6 snowflakes

Wooden Heart

The heart is one of the most popular folk art symbols. It is used in many countries, in all art mediums. This Czechoslovakian wooden heart would be a colorful addition to your Christmas tree.

MATERIALS AND TOOLS

Paper for pattern
Pencil
Scissors
$\frac{1}{8}$-inch plywood—4 x 4 inches
Jigsaw or coping saw
Sandpaper
Gesso
Paintbrush
Acrylic paints—red and assorted colors
Carbon paper
Drill with $\frac{1}{8}$-inch drill bit
Nylon fishing line for hanging

HOW TO MAKE

1. Trace the heart and its design onto paper to make a pattern (fig. 1). Cut out.

2. Place the paper pattern on the wood and trace the outline of the heart. Use a jigsaw or coping saw to cut out the wooden heart.

3. Smooth the edges with sandpaper.

4. Paint both sides of the heart with gesso to seal the wood. Let dry.

5. Paint the entire heart with a base coat of acrylic red. Let dry.

6. Transfer the heart design to the wood by placing a piece of carbon paper between the wood and the paper pattern. Then, trace the design on the pattern with a pencil.

7. Using bright, "peasant" colors, paint the design on the wood. Be sure to let one color dry completely before applying another color over it.

8. Drill a hole at the center top of the heart.

9. Thread a length of nylon fishing line through the hole and tie ends to make a loop for hanging.

FIG. 1   1 SQ. = $\frac{1}{2}$"

DENMARK

Elves

The Danish elf called Jul-Nisse is a kind elf but likes to play practical jokes and gets into all sorts of mischief. He helps with chores, tends the farm animals, and guards the household pets. He is usually with the household cat and is seen by no one except the cat. These little elves marry and have children and live in the attics of the farmhouses or in the lofts of the barns. The old Jul-Nisse of the family has long white whiskers and wears a red cap, long red stockings, and white clogs on his feet. It is customary on Christmas Eve for the children of the household to place porridge and a pitcher of milk outside the attic or barn door for the Jul-Nisse. The bowl is mysteriously empty by morning.

MATERIALS AND TOOLS

Wooden beads—natural-colored; round, oval, and cylindrical shapes
White glue—clear-drying
Paintbrush
Acrylic paints—red, green, blue
Pipe cleaners
Felt scraps—red, green
Lightweight yarn for hair
Polyester fiberfill for beards
Paper for patterns
Pencil
Ruler
Scissors
Tape measure
Straight pins
Burlap scraps—natural-colored
Purchased miniature accessories (optional)
Nylon fishing line for hanging

HOW TO MAKE

1. To make Jul-Nisse or any of his family, glue a round, wooden bead to an oval or cylindrical wooden bead to make a head and a body. Let dry.
2. Using acrylic paints, paint facial features on the round, natural-colored bead. See some suggested facial features in fig. 1.
3. Paint the body bead red, green, or blue. For hands, 2 small, natural-colored beads will be needed; however, for mittens, paint these small beads in the color of your choice. Let dry.
4. To make arms and hands/mittens, glue a small, round, wooden bead to each end of a length of pipe cleaner. Glue a narrow strip of felt (the same color as you painted the body) around the pipe cleaner (fig. 2). Let the felt dry before gluing the pipe cleaner around the body.

5. If you want hair to show on the elf, glue lengths of lightweight yarn to the head and let dry before styling it into braids, bun, or other hair style. For a beard, glue fiberfill to the face.
6. For a cap, make a paper pattern of a triangle with the base measuring about $\frac{1}{2}$ inch more than the distance around the wooden head. Draw the sides of the triangle so that when they are placed together, the cap will come to a point at the top. The sides of the triangle should overlap slightly.
7. Pin the paper pattern to felt and cut out. Slightly overlap and glue the edges of the sides of the felt triangle together forming a point at the top of the cap. Let dry before gluing the cap to the head. You may want to bend the top of the cap down and glue it to the side or back of the head.
8. The elf can wear a painted apron, a felt scarf, or a burlap shawl. You can also have him/her carry a paper Danish flag, a cardboard heart, a wrapped gift, a baby with a small bead head (wrapped in flannel and wearing a pointed cap), a burlap bag tied with yarn, a toothpick and raffia broom, or a birthday candle cut to size. For a decorative accessory, a miniature bell, lantern, or Christmas tree could be purchased.
9. Tie a length of nylon fishing line around the neck to make a loop for hanging.

FIG. 1

FIG. 2

Wood Shaving Ornaments

The Danish people are well known for their fine wooden handicrafts. Many of their Christmas ornaments make use of the natural textures of wood, wheat, and greenery.

MATERIALS AND TOOLS

Soft wood, such as pine—14 inches long, ¾ to 1 inch thick
Vise
Wood plane
Pencil
Ruler
Scissors
White glue—clear-drying
Bobby pins
Narrow ribbon or colored cord for hanging
Red felt scrap for elf's cap
Red cord, embroidery thread, or yarn for elf's belt
Polyester fiberfill for elf's beard
Paper for pattern
Straight pins
Artificial greenery for ball
Paper toweling
Colored cord or embroidery thread for star

HOW TO MAKE

1. Soak a 14-inch-long, ¾- to 1-inch-thick piece of soft wood, such as pine, in water for at least 8 hours. Clamp board in a vise and use a wood plane to cut several thin, 14-inch-long shavings. Soak the shavings in water about ½ hour to make them pliable. Use scissors to cut the shavings in half lengthwise to make ⅜-inch-wide strips. For each of these ornaments, the width of the strips will remain ⅜ inch but the lengths will vary.

2. When shaping and gluing these ornaments, use bobby pins to hold the strips in place. When dry, remove the bobby pins and attach a loop of narrow ribbon or colored cord to the top of the ornament for hanging.

HEART

Hearts are a traditional Christmas decoration in the Scandinavian countries.

1. Bend a 12-inch-long strip into a heart shape and glue the ends together. Roll a 2-inch-long strip into a circle and glue to the top of the heart (fig. 1).

ELF

This is a stylized likeness of Jul-Nisse (see page 80).

1. To make the body, bend a 13-inch-long strip in the middle; then bend the ends up to the waist and glue together, forming loops for legs (fig. 2).

2. Pinch the strip at the top to shape shoulders (fig. 3).

3. Roll a 2½-inch-long strip into a circle and glue on the shoulders for a head.

4. After the strips are dry, wrap red cord several times around the waist to make a belt and glue fiberfill to the chin for a beard.

5. Trace the cap shape to make a paper pattern (fig. 4). Pin the pattern to red felt and cut out. Roll the felt into a cone-shaped cap and secure with glue. Glue the cap to the head.

BIRD

1. To make the bird's body and tail, bend an 11-inch strip as shown. Secure with glue. Fringe the end of the tail with scissors (fig. 5).

2. Roll a 3-inch strip into a circle for a head and a 1-inch strip folded in the middle for a beak. Glue the beak to the head, then the head to the body (fig. 6).

BALL

1. Cut 2 strips, each 9 inches long. Bend each of the strips into a circle and glue to secure. Glue one circle inside the other to form a globe shape (fig. 7). Let dry. Glue artificial greenery to the top and bottom of the ball. Tie a narrow, red ribbon bow to the top.

STAR

1. Cut 4 short strips, each about 5 inches long. Place a dab of glue in the center of each strip; then cross one over the other, making 8 spokes (fig. 8). Place between paper towels and weight down until dry.

2. When dry, weave different colored cord or embroidery thread over and under the spokes covering about ½ inch out from the center. Secure the end with glue. Model the star further by cutting some of the spokes shorter than the others and cutting the ends of the spokes into different shapes (fig. 9).

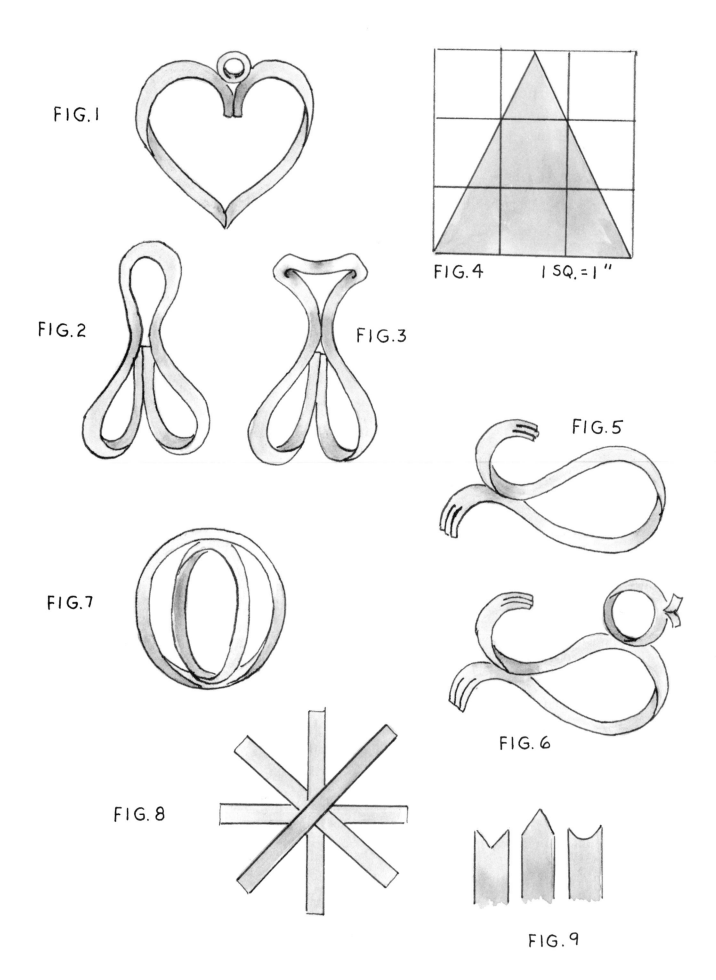

FIG.1

FIG.2

FIG.3

FIG.4   1 SQ. = 1"

FIG.5

FIG.6

FIG.7

FIG.8

FIG.9

ECUADOR

Bread Figures

The people of Ecuador have been making colorful, elegant bread-dough figures for hundreds of years. These figures were originally made as offerings of food for the dead and displayed at cemeteries on All Saints' Day. The tradition is still carried on today.

Over the years the making of bread-dough figures has evolved into a popular art form. Many different shapes are made—stars, birds, animals, people, and so on, with no two alike. Natural dyes are used to color the dough; then each tiny piece is shaped by hand and assembled. The finished figure is preserved with lacquer.

MATERIALS AND TOOLS

Bread slices
White glue—clear-drying
Bowl
Acrylic paints—assorted colors
Plastic sandwich bags
Waxed paper
Hand lotion (optional)
Paintbrush
Modeling implement, such as a toothpick, hairpin, or cuticle stick
Krylon Spray Fixative® (or other permanent protective coating)
Nylon fishing line for hanging

HOW TO MAKE

1. Mix the amount of dough that you think you will need for the shape you decide to make, using 1 tablespoon of white glue for each slice of bread. Remove all crusts; then break the bread into small pieces into a bowl. Add glue and knead until the mixture is smooth, soft, pliable, and no longer sticks to your hands.

2. Divide the dough into small balls. The number of balls depends on how many colors you will be using; however, keep 1 large ball uncolored. Knead acrylic paint into each ball until the dough is uniform in color. Use a different color for each ball. Place the balls in separate plastic bags. Keep the bags closed and take out only the amount of dough you will use each time, since air dries the dough. If it *does* dry, add a few drops of glue to moisten it.

3. Working on a sheet of waxed paper so the figure won't stick, shape a basic background form out of the uncolored dough flattened to about $\frac{1}{8}$-inch thick. For ease in handling the dough, put a small amount of hand lotion on your fingertips. Background shapes can be in the form of stars, turtles, clowns, witches, llamas, birds, etc. You will want to keep the finished figures small, about 3 or 4 inches high, so they will not be too heavy for tree ornaments.

4. Brush the basic shape with a mixture of $\frac{1}{2}$ glue and $\frac{1}{2}$ water, then build the basic shape up by adding small rolls, coils, cones, and balls of the colored dough. Use your imagination to pinch, squeeze, braid, layer, and mold the dough into details such as eyes, hair, rosettes, ruffles, etc. You can also imprint the surface with a toothpick, hairpin, small button, snap, etc.

5. Brush the finished figure with the glue/water mixture for minimum shrinkage and to prevent cracking.

6. Poke a small hole in the top of each figure. Thread a length of fishing line through the hole for hanging. Let the figure dry approximately 1 day.

7. Spray with a permanent protective coating.

8. You can store covered, unused dough in the refrigerator for several weeks.

ENGLAND

See: English Cracker, page 64.

FRANCE

See: French Pantin, page 70.

Wreath

MATERIALS AND TOOLS

Basket reed—fine
Raffia—natural-colored
Construction paper—red
Pencil
Scissors
White glue—clear-drying
Thread
4 stalks of wheat or dried grasses
Narrow red ribbon

HOW TO MAKE

1. Bend a 14-inch length of reed into a circle with a 4-inch diameter and secure with several rounds of raffia. Continue to wrap the raffia tightly around the entire reed a couple of times and tie to secure.

2. Trace the heart patterns onto red construction paper (fig. 1). Make 2 of each size. Cut out.

3. Glue the similar-sized hearts together, back to back, on each side of a length of thread. Tie one end of the thread to the top of the circle, letting the hearts hang free from the bottom and sides of the reed circle (fig. 2).

4. Tie 2 wheat stalks or dried grasses to either side of the top of the circle with raffia. Attach a narrow, red ribbon bow at the top and a loop of raffia for hanging (fig. 3).

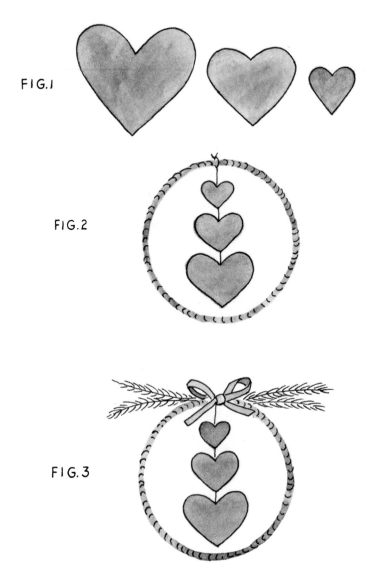

FIG.1

FIG.2

FIG.3

GERMANY

See also: German Cornucopia, page 63. See also: German Lebkuchen Cookies, page 67.

Pretzel Cookies

The biscuit pretzel was first made by monks in Southern Europe as a reward for children who learned their prayers. It was shaped to represent the crossed arms of a child praying. In Germany, pretzel-shaped cookies are baked for Christmas to hang on the tree.

INGREDIENTS

1 cup sugar
½ cup butter or margarine
2 eggs
2 one-ounce squares unsweetened chocolate, melted
1 teaspoon vanilla
2 cups sifted all-purpose flour
1½ teaspoons baking powder
½ teaspoon salt
½ teaspoon soda
¾ teaspoon cinnamon
¼ teaspoon ginger
¼ teaspoon allspice
Granulated sugar, to taste (to sprinkle on cookies)

MATERIALS AND TOOLS

Nylon fishing line for hanging

HOW TO MAKE

1. Cream sugar and butter or margarine, beating until fluffy. Add eggs, chocolate, and vanilla; beat well.
2. Sift dry ingredients together; stir into creamed mixture. Blend well. Wrap dough in plastic wrap or foil; refrigerate overnight.
3. To form pretzels, roll about 2 teaspoons dough with palms of hands on a lightly floured surface to form a 9-inch roll.
4. Pick up one end of the roll in each hand and cross over, forming a loop (fig. 1). Spread the ends apart and fold back onto the loop. Pinch the ends to the loop (fig. 2).
5. Sprinkle cookies with granulated sugar.
6. Using a wide spatula, gently transfer each cookie to an ungreased cookie sheet. Space 2 inches apart.
7. Bake at 350° F for 10 minutes until firm.

Yield: About 4 dozen cookies

FIG. 2

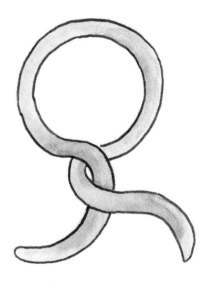

FIG. 1

Marzipan Candy

In Germany, the Christmas tree is decorated with candy called marzipan. This candy, made with almond paste, is molded into miniature, realistic-looking fruits, vegetables, figurines, toys, flowers, soap, sausages, and other humorous things. The German town of Lübeck in Northern Germany is famous for its realistic marzipan figures. One of the German traditions is to give little marzipan pigs to guests on New Year's Day to bring them good luck all year.

INGREDIENTS

1 can (8 ounces) almond paste (can be found in the baking goods section of your supermarket or a gourmet food market)
2 egg whites
½ teaspoon lemon extract
1 box (1 pound) powdered sugar
food coloring

MATERIALS AND TOOLS

Airtight plastic bags
Waxed paper
Pastry brush
Toothpick
Needle
Nylon fishing line for hanging

HOW TO MAKE

1. Break up the almond paste with your fingers into a medium-size bowl. Add 1 egg white, lemon extract, and about ½ cup powdered sugar; mix well. Knead in remaining sugar until mixture is smooth, firm, and malleable.

2. Divide the dough into as many pieces as you want colors. To color the pieces of dough, knead in drops of food coloring until a uniform shade is made. Place the pieces of colored dough in separate, airtight, plastic bags until ready to use so the dough doesn't dry out.

3. Cover the work surface with waxed paper. Shape all the parts of a figure first before joining them to make a complete figure (see fig. 1 for suggestions). To make the parts, roll pieces of dough between your palms to make small, smooth log shapes, pear shapes, balls, ovals, and cones. These parts can also be flattened, pinched, or sculpted to create desired shapes.

4. Join the parts of the figure by brushing some egg white where the parts meet and press in place, smoothing the seams.

5. Use your imagination to add details. A toothpick works well as a sculpturing tool to make lines, ridges, creases, and textures.

6. Let the completed figure dry about 1 hour before attaching a thread for hanging.

7. Thread a needle with nylon fishing line and insert through the top of the figure. Tie the ends in a knot to make a loop for hanging. Wait until the figure is dry and firm before hanging it on the tree.

FIG. 1

Toadstool

Southern Germany's Black Forest is a paradise for mushroom hunters. This brightly colored papier mâché toadstool is considered a symbol of good luck in Germany.

MATERIALS AND TOOLS

Pencil
Ruler
Scissors
Newspaper
Masking tape
Florist's wire—22 gauge to make loop for hanging
Waxed paper
Paintbrush
Gesso
Acrylic paints—red, white
Paper toweling
Metylan Art Paste (or other mâché paste)
Krylon Spray Fixative® (or other permanent protective coating)

HOW TO MAKE

1. To form the cap of the mushroom, crush an 11 x 14-inch piece of newspaper into a ball. Flatten and shape it until it is about 3 inches in diameter. Use masking tape to hold it in shape.

2. To form the stem, crush a 7 x 11-inch piece of newspaper into a cylinder about 1½ inches high. Twist to make a gnarled stem. Hold with masking tape.

3. Attach the stem to the cap with masking tape.

4. Insert the twisted ends of a loop of florist's wire into the top of the mushroom for hanging the ornament after it is completed.

5. Working on waxed paper, tear paper toweling into ¾ x 2-inch strips. Dip each strip into mâché paste. Wring it by gently sliding it between 2 fingers; then smooth it over the mushroom. Cover the mushroom completely with at least 2 layers, slightly overlapping the strips. Let dry.

6. Apply a coat of gesso. Let dry.

7. Using acrylic paints, paint the cap red with irregular white circles. Paint the stem white. Let dry.

8. Spray with a permanent protective coating.

INDIA

Mirrored Cloth Figures

These colorful stuffed animals and doll are adaptations of the famous mirrored cloth art work of the Saurashtra region of India, *shishadur*. This mirrorwork is used on clothing, wall hangings, and the blankets of oxen that pull carts.

MATERIALS AND TOOLS

Paper for patterns
Pencil
Scissors
Felt—assorted colors
Needle
Thread—various colors
Gold braid
Colored metallic trims—spangles, glitter, sequins
Polyester fiberfill
Crochet hook (optional)
Gold thread for hanging

HOW TO MAKE

1. Enlarge and trace 1 or all of the figure shapes onto paper (fig. 1). Cut out.

2. Place the paper pattern on a piece of colored felt and cut out 2 of the same shape to make a front and a back.

3. Using needle and thread, appliqué small felt pieces of a contrasting color to the front piece to make an eye, mouth, and other decorative accents.

4. Sew on gold braid, gold thread, and a variety of colored metallic trims to add glittering color to the ornament.

5. Stitch the front and back pieces together, using a running stitch. Be careful not to stretch one piece more than the other (see fig. 2). Leave a small opening for stuffing.

6. Stuff the ornament with polyester fiberfill. A crochet hook is handy for reaching tiny places. Sew the opening closed.

7. Add a length of looped gold thread for hanging.

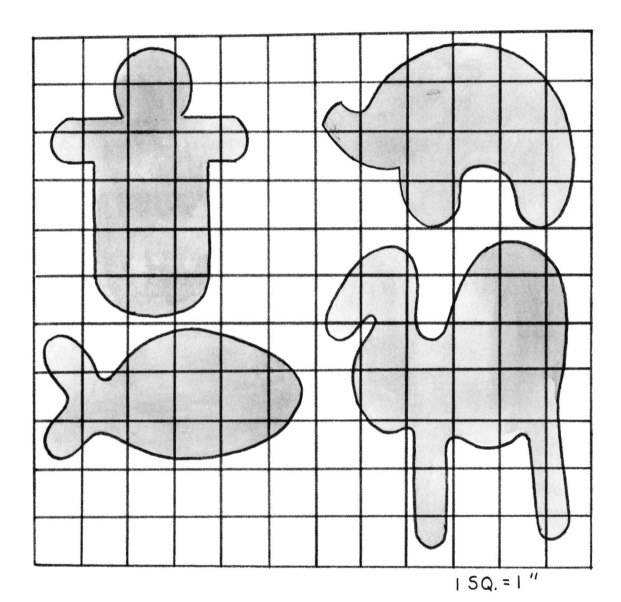

FIG.1

1 SQ. = 1"

FIG. 2

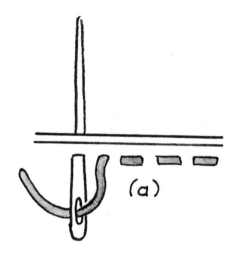

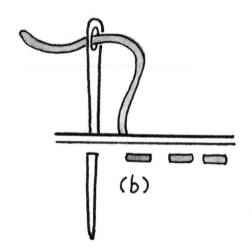

INSERT NEEDLE
AT RIGHT ANGLES
TO THE EDGES OF
MATERIAL FROM
FRONT TO BACK
AND THEN FROM
BACK TO FRONT

IRELAND

Leprechaun

One of the traditional figures of Irish folklore is the leprechaun. The leprechaun is a cranky, wrinkled, little, old man who makes shoes for the fairies. If captured, he buys his freedom by telling (falsely) where he has hidden his pot of gold.

MATERIALS AND TOOLS

Two 12-inch-long pink chenille stems
Scissors
Green yarn
White glue—clear-drying

Compass
Felt—green, pink
Embroidery thread—blue, red, brown, white
Needle
Thread
Polyester fiberfill

HOW TO MAKE

1. Fold a 12-inch length of pink chenille stem in half, shaping a circle for a head. Then, twist it about 3 or 4 times to form a torso. Leave the remaining ends of the chenille stem for legs. Bend the legs at the knees and turn up the ends for feet (fig. 1).

2. Make arms by twisting a 6-inch length of pink chenille stem a couple of times around the upper part of the torso. Bend the arms at the elbows and turn up the ends for hands (fig. 2).

3. With the exception of the head and hands, wrap the entire figure with green yarn. Glue down the ends.

4. To make the face and the back of the head, cut 2 circles with 1½-inch diameters from pink felt.

5. Embroider facial features on one of the pink felt pieces. Use a satin stitch to make white eyes with blue pupils. Also, outline the eyes with the blue. Stitch a red mouth and brown eyebrows (fig. 3).

6. Place the embroidered face over the front of the chenille head and the other circle of pink felt behind the chenille head. Sew the 2 pieces together, leaving an opening large enough to stuff with fiberfill; then sew the opening closed.

7. Use the pattern to cut a hat from green felt (fig. 4). Stitch the front of the hat around the face; continue stitching up the back of the hat to shape it into a cone.

8. Glue on a fiberfill beard. Twist the leprechaun in a position to hang, sit, or lie on the Christmas tree.

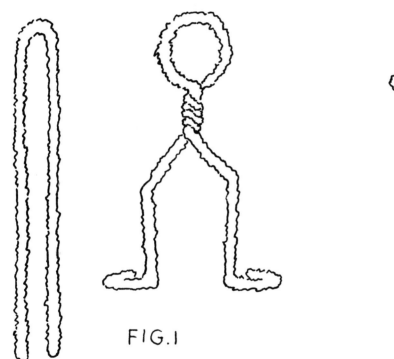

FIG. 1

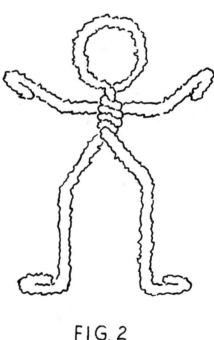

FIG. 2

FIG. 3

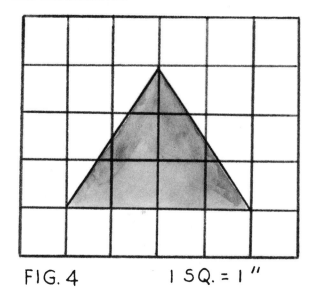

FIG. 4   1 SQ. = 1"

ITALY

Befana the Christmas Witch, or, Babouschka the Russian Christmas Witch

Befana, a benevolent old witch, is Italy's "Santa Claus," who rides from house to house on a broomstick. Over her shoulder, she carries a bag filled with candy and gifts for good children and pieces of charcoal for the naughty ones. She also carries in her hand a bell that she rings to announce her arrival at each house. The origin of Befana is explained in a Christmas legend that tells of her refusal to help the Wise Men when they questioned her about directions to Bethlehem. She later repented and set out to find them. Failing to find the Wise Men, she has continued to wander about, rewarding good children with presents but leaving charcoal for children who deserve punishment.

Russia has a similar but sadder legend. Babouschka too is an old woman who laments her refusal to assist the Wise Men. Ever since, she has hurried about at Christmas, going into each home, looking into every cradle for the Christ Child. Not finding him, she drops a tear, leaves gifts for the good children, and continues her search.

MATERIALS AND TOOLS

Chenille stems—two 12-inch-long lengths
Nylon pantyhose or stockings
Compass
Scissors
Polyester fiberfill
Long needle
Thread
Ruler
Fabric scraps
Yarn—gray and either red or green

Paper for patterns
Pencil
Small black beads for eyes
Black felt
Burlap
Small hand bell (can be purchased from craft and hobby shops)
$\frac{1}{8}$-inch wooden dowel or $7\frac{1}{2}$-inch-long twig for broomstick
Straw, raffia, or shredded corn husk for broom
String
Nylon fishing line for hanging

HOW TO MAKE

1. To make the body, line up two 12-inch-long chenille stems side by side, parallel to each other. Leaving the top 3 inches untwisted for arms, twist the 2 stems together to form a torso. Leave the bottom 3 inches of the stems untwisted for legs (fig. 1).

2. To make the neck, twist the 3-inch-long arms down over the torso for about ¾ inch (fig. 2).

3. To make the head, cut a circle with a 3-inch diameter from a nylon stocking. Baste around the outside of the nylon circle. Place stuffing into the center of the basted nylon circle. Then, pull the thread to gather the nylon around the stuffing (fig. 3). Fit the chenille stem neck into the head opening; then pull the thread tightly around the neck and knot.

4. To give fullness to the arms and legs, wrap stuffing around each chenille arm and leg; bind with thread (fig. 4).

5. Cover the stuffing with nylon strips long enough to cover each arm and leg. Stitch with matching thread to hold snugly.

6. To make facial features, thread a long needle and knot. Pass the needle from the back of the head to the front, coming through at the top of the nose area, and to one side. Stitch back and forth, pushing the needle under a tuft of stuffing with each stitch. Shape the nose by working downward and gradually increasing the distance between the stitches. Use your fingers to pinch narrow ridges of the nylon-covered stuffing to shape eyebrows and lips; then stitch back and forth, using small stitches to hold the ridges in place.

7. To make the dress, cut fabric scraps as follows—two 4-inch squares for the sleeves, one 3 x 5-inch rectangle for the bodice, and one 5 x 10-inch rectangle for the skirt (fig. 5). Hem both longer sides of the bodice and skirt and the 2 opposite sides of each sleeve.

8. With right sides facing, seam the raw edges of the bodice, making a tube. Do the same to make a tube for each sleeve and 1 for the skirt. Turn the tubes right-side-out and slip the bodice and sleeves on the body. Keep the seams at the back of the bodice and at the underarms of the sleeves. Stitch the top of the bodice to the neck and the sleeves to the bodice, folding raw edges under and taking tucks when necessary.

9. Using fiberfill, stuff the chest area through the waist opening. Gather the edges of the openings tightly to close around the hands and waist. Tie with thread.

10. Baste around the top edge of the skirt tube. Slip the tube on the body. Pull the gathers tight; then stitch the skirt to the bottom of the bodice, turning the raw edge of the bodice under.

11. To make hair, cut approximately ten 6-inch lengths of gray yarn. Place the yarn over the head and stitch to make a center part (fig. 6). Gently brush the yarn to make it fuzzy.

12. Turn up the ends of the chenille stem legs to make feet. Make a paper shoe pattern. Fold a piece of black felt in half and place the heel of the paper pattern on the fold; cut out (fig. 7). Repeat for the other shoe. Glue in place around each foot.

13. To make the cape, cut a 6-inch square from black felt. Sew a ¼-inch casing along one edge. Thread a length of yarn or ribbon through the casing, gather tightly around the neck, and tie in a bow.

14. To make the hat, cut a triangle of black felt 4½ inches on 2 sides and 6 inches on the third side (fig. 8). Fold the hat in half; then sew the 4½-inch edges together. Cut to round the bottom edge of the hat (fig. 9). Turn the hat inside out and stuff with fiberfill. Glue the hat to the head, positioning the seam to the center back.

15. To make the bag, cut a 4 x 6-inch piece of burlap. Sew a narrow hem along one long edge for the top of the bag. Fold the burlap with right sides facing and stitch the 2 short sides together and then sew the bottom seam. Turn right-side-out, stuff with fiberfill; then gather the top of the bag together with a length of red or green yarn tied in a bow. Stitch the bag to one of the hands.

16. Stitch a small bell to the other hand.

17. To make the broom, cut a 7½-inch length of wooden doweling or use a twig. Tie raffia, straw, or shredded strips of corn husks to one end.

18. Attach the broomstick to the body by twisting the chenille legs around the broomstick and tying securely in place with string.

19. Thread a length of nylon fishing line through the back of the hat to make a loop for hanging.

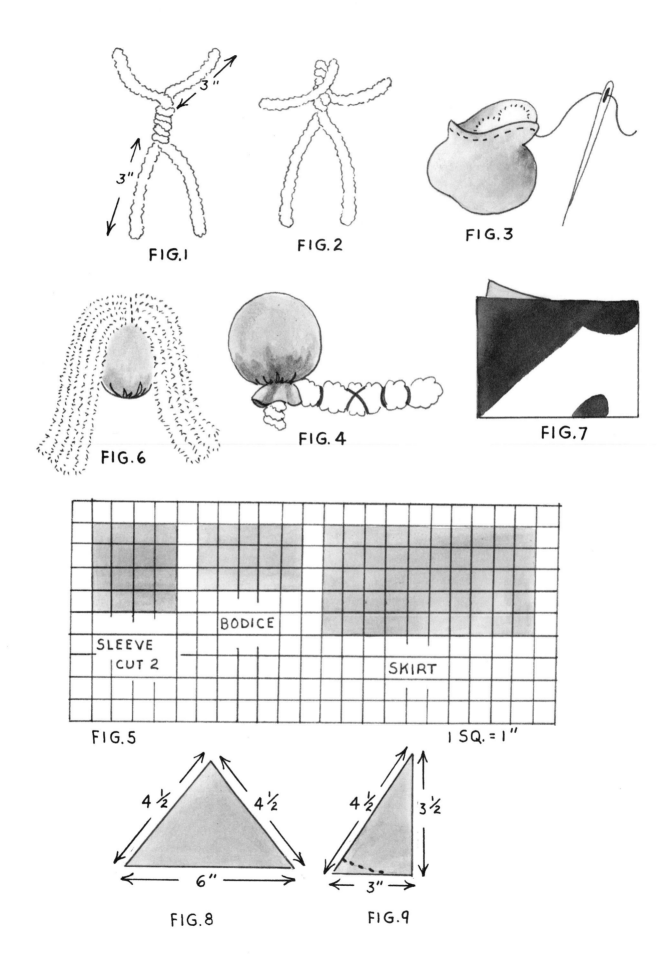

FIG.1

FIG.2

FIG.3

FIG.6

FIG.4

FIG.7

SLEEVE
CUT 2

BODICE

SKIRT

FIG.5

1 SQ. = 1"

4½   4½

6"

FIG.8

4½   3½

3"

FIG.9

JAPAN

Kokeshi Doll

This very stylized Japanese doll is made with a large, round, wooden head resting on a long, cylindrical, wooden body. To keep the simplicity of the doll, it is made without arms or legs. Lips, eyes, and eyebrows are painted on the head, and flowers are usually painted on the body.

Kokeshi dolls were first made about 300 years ago in Tohoku, a mountainous region in northeast Japan. Their origin is not known, but they may have had a religious purpose. It is believed that the dolls may have been presented at shrines by worshipers to guarantee the prosperity of their descendants. In Japan, dolls were once thought to house ancestral spirits or dieties, and, therefore, were believed to have magical powers. Today, the Kokeshi doll is a plaything and is sold primarily as a gift.

MATERIALS AND TOOLS

Wooden beads—natural-colored; round, oval, and cylindrical shapes
White glue—clear-drying
Weldwood® Wood Filler, Plastic Wood® or other wood filler (check in hardware or lumber stores)
Paintbrush
Acrylic paints—assorted colors
Metallic gold thread or nylon fishing line for hanging

HOW TO MAKE

1. Glue a round, wooden bead to an oval or cylindrical wooden bead to make a head and body. Let dry.

2. Fill the hole at the top of the round bead with wood filler (Plastic Wood®). Let dry.

3. Using acrylic paints, paint black hair, eyes, and nose on the round bead. Paint a red mouth. See suggested facial features (fig. 1). Let dry.

4. Paint the oval or cylindrical wooden bead to resemble a Japanese kimono. See suggested designs (fig. 2). Let dry.

5. Tie a length of metallic gold thread or nylon fishing line around the neck to make a loop for hanging.

FIG. 1

FIG. 2

Thread Ball

The thread ball is a Japanese folk toy originally used for games at court. This ball is traditionally made of paper covered with thread and then embroidered with beautiful designs.

MATERIALS AND TOOLS

3-inch plastic-foam ball
Crochet thread—black cotton, 1 skein (100 yards)
White glue—clear-drying
Needle
Embroidery thread—various bright colors
Scissors
Cardboard—2 x 6 inches

HOW TO MAKE

1. For convenience, use a plastic-foam ball rather than a paper ball. Glue one end of a skein of black crochet thread to the ball and wrap the thread around the ball 6 to 10 times in one direction, then 6 to 10 times in another direction. Continue, changing directions until the ball is completely covered. Glue the end down.

2. Thread a needle with embroidery thread and begin to embroider simple, colorful, geometric designs onto the black crochet thread. Use a combination of bright colors for the design. Tuck all knots under the black crochet thread.

3. To make a tassel to hang from the bottom of the ball, wind embroidery thread 12 times around a 6-inch-long piece of cardboard. Slip a length of embroidery thread through the loops at one edge of the cardboard and tie the strands tightly together, leaving at least 3-inch ends (fig. 1). Cut the loops at the other edge. Tie a length of embroidery thread tightly around the strands, about $\frac{1}{2}$ inch below the top (fig. 2). Trim the ends of the tassel to a uniform length.

4. Sew the tassel to the bottom of the ball. Finish by attaching a loop of embroidery thread through the top of the ball for hanging.

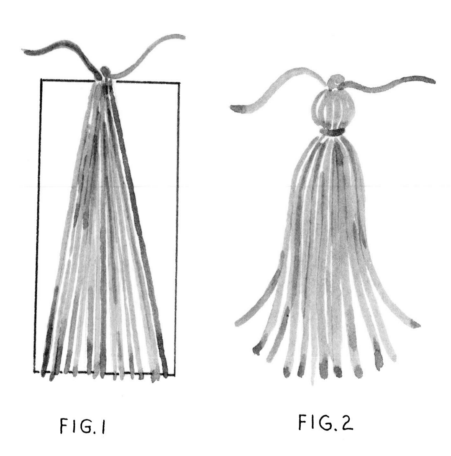

FIG. 1   FIG. 2

Fan

Silk and paper fans have been an important handicraft in Japan for centuries. In the 1890's, it was fashionable in American cities to purchase a variety of inexpensive party favors and ornaments such as parasols, lanterns, and fans from Japanese stores to decorate the late Victorian Christmas tree.

MATERIALS AND TOOLS

Lightweight cardboard or poster board—3 x 3 inches
Scissors
Felt pens—permanent, fine-tipped
White glue—clear-drying
Popsicle or craft stick
Paintbrush
Acrylic paint
Krylon Spray Fixative® (or other permanent protective coating)
Embroidery thread (for tassel)

HOW TO MAKE

1. Cut 2 identical shapes from a 3-inch square of lightweight cardboard or poster board, either oval or heart-shaped but with a very rounded point.

2. Glue a picture with an oriental motif onto the cardboard or paint an oriental picture using felt pens. See Kokeshi Doll (page 96) for suggested oriental designs.

3. Paint a popsicle stick or craft stick black. Let dry, then glue it between the 2 cardboard shapes for a handle.

4. Spray the fan with a permanent protective coating.

5. Make a hole at the bottom of the handle to tie a tassel. To make a tassel, see Thread Ball (page 97).

Carp (Koniburo)

On May 5th, the day of the "Boys' Festival," every family in Japan that has a son hangs a brilliantly painted cloth or paper carp from a bamboo pole. The carp acts as a windsock and the wind makes it look as if it were swimming upstream. The carp's fight upstream against swift currents to lay its eggs makes it Japan's symbol of courage, ambition, and perseverance. The flying of the Koniburo is a way of inspiring Japanese children.

MATERIALS AND TOOLS

White, 100% cotton fabric—9 x 12 inches
Paper for pattern
Pencil
Scissors
Sturdy cardboard
Masking tape
Vogart® Ball Point fabric paints
Needle
Thread for sewing—white
Florist's wire—22 gauge to reinforce mouth
Gold thread for hanging (10-inch length)

HOW TO MAKE

1. Wash and iron a 9 x 12-inch piece of white, 100% cotton fabric. Stretch the fabric tightly and smoothly over a piece of sturdy cardboard. Hold it down with masking tape.

2. Enlarge the fish shape to make a paper pattern (fig. 1).

3. Cut out the paper pattern and place it on the fabric, laying out so that there is room for 2 shapes. Trace around the outside of the pattern lightly with a pencil; then lift and turn the pattern over. Trace around it again to make a second half.

4. Draw the eyes, scales, and other designs on both halves of the fabric lightly with pencil before painting with the fabric paints (fig. 2). Let paint dry thoroughly before removing the fabric from the cardboard.

5. Cut out the 2 halves of the painted carp. With right sides facing, sew around the carp, leaving the mouth and tail sections open (fig. 3).

6. Turn right-side-out and fold up the raw edge around the tail. Glue to hold in place.

7. Cut a 4-inch length of florist's wire. Bend it into a circle and place inside the mouth. Fold raw edge of the fabric back over wire and glue in place (fig. 4).

8. Thread the ends of a 10-inch length of gold thread through both sides of the mouth, keeping the knots inside the mouth, to make a loop for hanging.

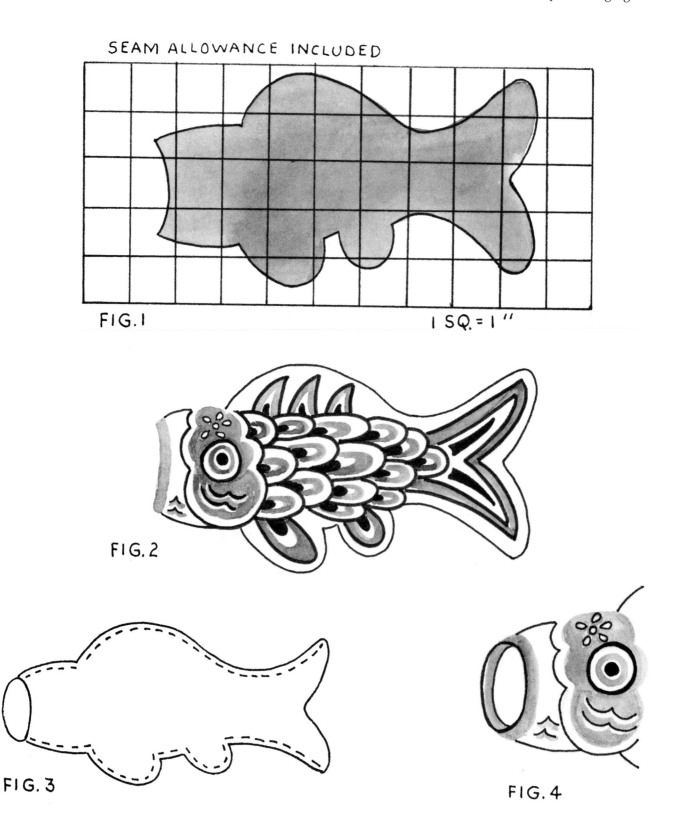

SEAM ALLOWANCE INCLUDED

FIG. 1

1 SQ. = 1"

FIG. 2

FIG. 3

FIG. 4

Hatiman Doll

This traditional Japanese doll is made from papier mâché and decorated with pine, bamboo, and plum blossom designs.

Most Japanese folk toys were first made in an age when science was not advanced. A large number became popular because of a superstitious belief in their power to confer good or bad luck. The Hatiman doll may be regarded as a toy doll or a charm. It is weighted at the bottom. When it is knocked down, it rights itself immediately, showing courageous resistance and final success. This characteristic has made the Hatiman doll a symbol of good luck.

In Japan it is customary to give this doll as a New Year's gift or as a farewell present.

MATERIALS AND TOOLS

Aluminum foil
Florist's wire—22 gauge to make loop for hanging
Waxed paper
Activa® Products, Inc. Celluclay
Paintbrush
Gesso
Acrylic paints—assorted colors
Krylon Spray Fixative® (or other permanent protective coating)

HOW TO MAKE

1. Crumble and mold a sheet of aluminum foil into a pear-shaped figure about 4 inches high and 3½ inches wide at the widest point.

2. Insert the twisted ends of a loop of florist's wire into the top of the figure for hanging the ornament after it is completed.

3. Work on waxed paper. Using Celluclay, fill any holes made by crushing the foil; then cover and shape the entire figure with a thin, smooth layer of Celluclay. Keep your finger moistened with water for easier smoothing. Let the figure dry.

4. Apply a coat of gesso to the complete figure. Let dry.

5. Using acrylic paints, paint the doll red with a white face. Let dry, then paint the eyes, eyebrows, and nose black, the mouth red, and the design on the front of the doll's kimono as shown (fig. 1).

6. Spray the doll with a permanent protective coating.

FIG.1

Daruma Doll

The Daruma doll is symbolic of an Indian monk called Dharma, the legendary founder of Zen Buddhism who believed that one should seek inner security and a balanced, ordered life. This doll is the most common papier mâché toy in Japan and is usually made in the form of a male figure. It has a rounded, hollow body and is so weighted that whenever it is pushed over, it always rights itself. According to legend, Dharma's years of constant meditation caused his limbs to shrivel away, so this doll is always made without arms and legs. There is a tradition in Japan that when you make a wish you paint one eye on the Daruma doll, and when your wish comes true you paint in the other eye.

The materials, tools, and directions on how to make this doll are the same as those for the Japanese Hatiman Doll (page 101), with the exception of the painting. See fig. 1 for the correct patterns to paint. There is no need to weight the doll if it is to be used as a Christmas tree ornament.

FIG. 1

Origami Peacock

The Japanese paper sculpture called "origami" is a paper-folding art believed to have originated in China in the seventh century. Origami peacocks make novel Christmas tree ornaments.

MATERIALS AND TOOLS

Colored origami paper (or any light paper that keeps its folds)
Ruler

Pencil
Scissors
White glue—clear-drying
Florist's pick with wire attached

HOW TO MAKE

1. With the brightly colored side facing out, fold a 6-inch square of paper in half, on the diagonal, to make a crease, then open (fig. 1).

2. Fold the 2 sides over so that they join at the crease (fig. 2).

3. Turn the paper over so that the brightly colored side is facing you. Measure down the center crease $3\frac{3}{4}$ inches from the top point and mark a dot lightly with pencil. Measure down each of the outside edges $2\frac{1}{2}$ inches from the top edge and mark with dots. Lightly draw lines connecting the dot on the crease to each of the dots on the edges to make 2 lines to guide you in folding (fig. 3). Fold the paper on the drawn lines (fig. 4).

4. Open the paper to the position you had for figure 3. This time, measure down the center crease only $2\frac{3}{4}$ inches from the top point and mark a dot. Measure down the outside edges only $1\frac{3}{4}$ inches and mark dots.

Draw lines connecting the dots as you did in step 3 (fig. 5). Pinch the center crease together to make it easier to fold the paper on the drawn lines so that the point turns up (fig. 6).

5. Once again open the paper to the position you had for figure 3. Measure down the center crease only 1 inch from the top point and mark a dot. Measure down the outside edges only $\frac{3}{4}$ inches and mark dots. Draw lines connecting the dots (fig. 7). Fold the paper on the drawn lines so that the point turns down to make a head (fig. 8).

6. Cut a tail design along the bottom (fig. 9).

7. From contrasting colored papers, design and cut a tuft of "feathers." Glue to the top of the head. Glue on small round circles for eyes. Add brightly colored concentric circles or ovals to decorate the tail (fig. 10).

8. Glue, then insert the pointed end of a florist's pick up into the head, leaving the wire at the bottom for attaching the peacock to a tree branch.

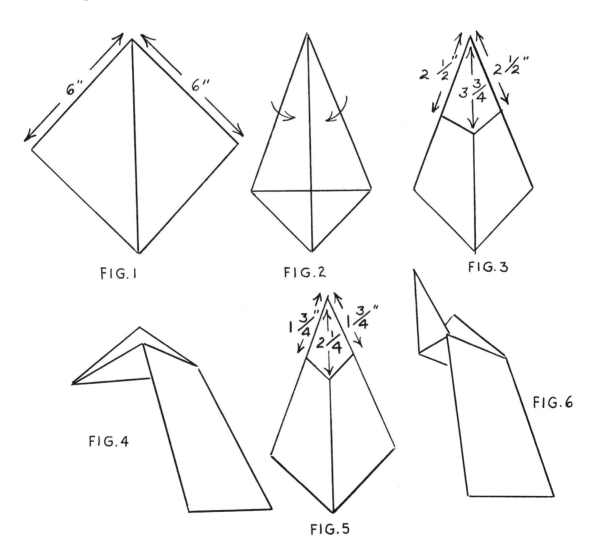

FIG. 1

FIG. 2

FIG. 3

FIG. 4

FIG. 5

FIG. 6

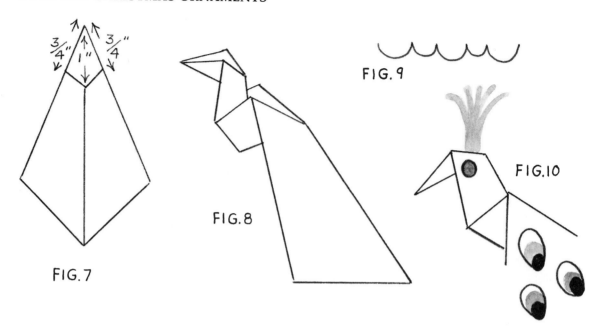

FIG.7

FIG.8

FIG.9

FIG.10

Beckoning Cat

The beckoning cat was originally sold at temples, and it was believed that prosperity and good fortune would come to a person who kept a cat. Since then, the cat has often been placed in homes and shops to summon good luck. It is usually made of clay with a white body and black facial features and whiskers.

Use the same materials, tools, and directions as for the Mexican Clay Figures (see page 109), but paint as shown in figure 1.

FIG.1

LITHUANIA

Bird

Suspended from a Christmas tree and with the slightest movement of air, this tiny, light-weight bird, made from a walnut shell and feathers, gives the impression that it's flying.

MATERIALS AND TOOLS

Walnut for body
Knife
Feathers
White glue—clear-drying
Pod for head
Felt pen—black, fine-tipped
Nylon fishing line for hanging

HOW TO MAKE

1. Heat a walnut in a 300° F oven for 20 minutes or until the shell can be pried open easily when the tip of a knife blade is inserted. Empty the nut of its meats.

2. On the rim of 1 half-shell, glue feathers for wings and a tail. Also, glue the ends of a length of nylon fishing line to the rim on opposite sides to make a loop for hanging (fig. 1).

3. Seal the 2 halves of the shell together with glue.

4. Glue a small pod, with the stem attached, to the walnut, making a head and a beak. Paint small, black dots with a felt pen for eyes (fig. 2).

FIG.1

FIG. 2

MEXICO

Hobby Horse

Mexican folk art shops are filled at Christmas time with colorful, inexpensive papier mâché toys. Toys made from the same mold can look entirely different because of the varied, vivid, and gay colors the Mexican artist may use. For example, the same-shaped burro may be painted red, pink, or purple.

MATERIALS AND TOOLS

Aluminum foil
Wooden skewer or lollipop stick
White glue—clear-drying
Waxed paper
Activa® Products Celluclay
Paintbrush
Gesso
Acrylic paints—assorted colors
Krylon Spray Fixative® (or other permanent protective coating)
Yarn for reins

HOW TO MAKE

1. Crush a piece of aluminum foil into the shape of a horse's head and neck (fig. 1).

2. Glue a wooden skewer or lollipop stick into the neck far enough to secure it to the horse.

3. Working on waxed paper, cover the head and neck with a smooth layer of Celluclay. Build up ears with the Celluclay. Keep your finger moistened with water for easier smoothing. Let dry.

4. Apply a coat of gesso. Let dry.

5. Using acrylic paints, decorate the horse in contrasting, brilliant colors. Let dry.

6. Spray the horse with a permanent protective coating.

7. Glue a loop of yarn around the horse's neck to make reins for hanging.

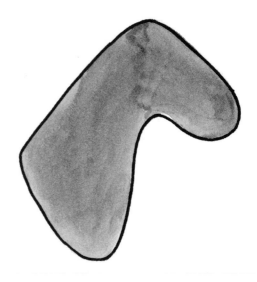

FIG. 1

Piñata

The piñata is a paper-wrapped earthen jar filled with sweets and small toys. It is often decorated to resemble a bird or other creature. A traditional Christmas-time festivity in Mexico is the Los Posados ceremony: Children go from house to house on each of the nine nights before Christmas seeking lodging, as did Mary and Joseph. When they are admitted, a piñata is waiting for them. The piñata is hung by a cord from the ceiling. The children are blindfolded and take turns trying to break the piñata with a stick. When it breaks, the gifts and candies fall to the ground, and all the children scramble after them.

The instructions given here are for an adaptation of the traditional piñata. It is made to hold little gifts and candies on the tree and can be used year after year.

MATERIALS AND TOOLS

Florist's wire—22 gauge to make loop for hanging
Masking tape
L'eggs® hose plastic egg container
Paper toweling
Metylan Art Paste (or other mâché paste)
White glue—clear-drying
Ruler
Pencil
Scissors
Tissue paper—bright colors of your choice
Yarn, cord, or ribbon for hanging

HOW TO MAKE

1. Bend a short length of florist's wire in half and twist the ends to make a loop for hanging. Tape the wire ends to secure them in place on top of the plastic egg (fig. 1).

2. Cover the outside of the egg, including the wire ends of the loop, with small, torn strips of paper toweling dipped in mâché paste. Do not put any paste-covered strips over the seams where the plastic egg halves join so that you will be able to open the egg after the piñata is completed. Slide each strip between 2 fingers to free it of any excess paste before smoothing it onto the egg. Overlap the strips. Apply at least 2 layers of strips; then, allow the egg to dry completely. If the dried mâché form pulls away from the plastic egg, glue it back in place.

3. Cut tissue-paper strips 2 inches wide and 30 inches long. Fold each strip in half lengthwise. Fringe by cutting from the folded edge to within ½ inch of the opposite edge. Make your cuts about ⅛ inch apart (fig. 2).

4. Turn each strip inside out so the fringe pops out. Working on one-half of the egg at a time, glue the fringe to the egg, overlapping the rows (fig. 3).

5. Cut several ¼ x 10-inch-long streamers and glue to the bottom of the egg.

6. Attach yarn, cord, or ribbon to the wire loop at the top of the piñata for hanging.

FIG. 1

FIG. 3

FIG. 2

Indian "Eye of God" (*Ojo de Dios*)

The colorful talisman called "Eye of God" is borrowed from the ancient traditions of the Indians of Mexico, Central America, and Southwestern United States. The talismans symbolize good luck, good fortune, good health, and a long, happy life. They are made in various colors and designs with the central eye in the center representing the eye of the universe. Although they were not originally made for Christmas, they make colorful, attractive tree decorations.

MATERIALS AND TOOLS

¼-inch wooden dowel—two 6-inch lengths
Saw
Craft knife
White glue—clear-drying
4-ply knitting yarn—various colors
Scissors

HOW TO MAKE

1. Cut two 6-inch lengths from a ¼-inch dowel. Using a knife, notch the centers of the 2 dowels and glue together to make a cross (fig. 1). Let dry.

2. Knot a length of yarn around the center where the dowels cross. Begin winding the yarn over the top of each spoke, around the back of it, then over the top of the next one, always in the same counter-clockwise direction (fig. 2). Continue until there is an "eye" about the size you'd like. Be sure to keep the yarn taut as you wind.

3. Change colors whenever you like. To change colors, cut the yarn, leaving an end to tuck under later. Begin by winding the new yarn twice around the spoke, again leaving an end that can be tucked in later. Produce accents by making rings of different widths with different colors.

4. To get a three-dimensional or see-through effect, wind awhile on one side, then turn the cross over and wind in the same direction so that the design is sometimes on one side, sometimes on the other.

5. For star points, wind yarn around the opposite ends of one dowel; repeat on the second dowel. Return to a square pattern by winding around all 4 spokes.

6. When you come to the end of the design, secure the final piece of yarn with a dab of glue.

7. To make a tassel for each of the 4 ends of the dowels, wrap yarn around 4 fingers (or a piece of cardboard 2½ to 3 inches wide) about 15 times. Loop together at one end with a piece of yarn (fig. 3). Tie the tassel to the end of the dowel with the loop ends. Distribute the yarn evenly around the dowel. Secure the tassel with a dab of glue and 2 more pieces of yarn, spaced ½ inch apart (fig. 4). Cut, then trim the loops.

8. Tie a length of yarn around a dowel at the base of 1 tassel to make a loop for hanging.

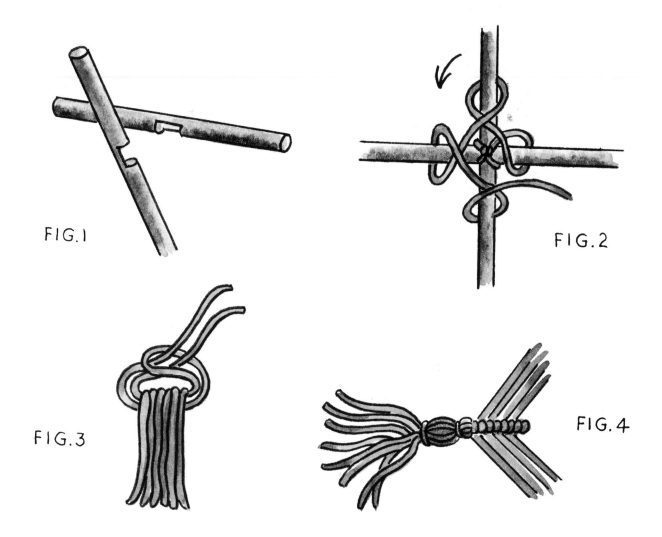

FIG. 1

FIG. 2

FIG. 3

FIG. 4

Clay Figures

Many of the cities and towns in Mexico specialize in producing certain kinds of clay figures. The stylized clay animal and bird figures may be painted with subtle earth colors, painted with brilliant colors, or left in their natural state.

MATERIALS AND TOOLS

Westwood® Ovencraft Clay (can be found in hobby and craft stores)
Plastic bag
Modeling tools—toothpick, popsicle stick, small knife
Paintbrush
Acrylic paints—assorted colors
Krylon Spray Fixative® (or other permanent protective coating)
Florist's wire—22 gauge to make loop for hanging
White glue—clear-drying

HOW TO MAKE

1. Keep the clay figure small, about 2 to 3 inches long and no thicker than 1 inch at any point. Also, keep the figure simple and free of detail, making only the essential characteristics (fig. 1).

2. Keep unused clay in a plastic bag to keep it moist and workable. To delay drying while you're working, dampen your hands with water.

3. Begin with a lump of clay, pulling out the clay to form a head, legs, or other appendages, depending upon the figure. Squeeze, pinch, and push the clay to shape the figure further. Keep the parts chunky so they will not break off easily. Parts can also be made separately and joined while they are moist. To do this, roughen both joining surfaces by scratching them with a toothpick. Spread the roughened surfaces with water; then press the scratched parts together. Weld them together with a tool or your fingertip.

4. Smooth the figure by dipping your finger in water and rubbing it over the figure.

5. Poke a small hole in the center top of the figure to be used later for a wire loop for hanging.

6. If your figure is not finished in 1 working period, cover it with a damp cloth and plastic so it will stay airtight.

7. Allow the clay figure to dry and harden at room temperature. Turn the figure frequently so that it dries evenly. Drying time can vary from a few hours to several days, depending on size, thickness, and room humidity.

8. When the figure is completely dry, place it in a cold oven and bring the temperature up to 350° F. Average baking time is 1 hour.

9. Using acrylic paints, paint your figure with subtle earth colors or with brilliant colors. See the Mexican designs suggested under Mexican "Tin" Ornaments (page 112). Let dry.

10. Spray the figure with a permanent protective coating.

11. For hanging, fold a short length of florist's wire in half and twist the ends together to form a loop. Place glue into the hole at the top center of the figure. Insert the twisted end of the wire into the hole.

FIG.1

Charro Hat

This hat—along with an elaborately decorated cowboy suit, a bolero jacket, and tight trousers—is the national costume for Mexican men.

MATERIALS AND TOOLS

Compass
Paper for patterns
Pencil
Straight pins
Black felt
Scissors
Needle
Thread—black
Polyester fiberfill
Silver braid
White glue—clear-drying
Silver sequins
Yarn—lightweight, black
Small black bead

HOW TO MAKE

1. Using a compass, draw a circle with a 3-inch diameter on paper to make a pattern for the hat brim.
2. Pin the paper pattern to a piece of black felt and cut out 2 felt pieces. Sew the edges of the 2 felt pieces together with an overcast stitch to make a brim (fig. 1).
3. Enlarge and trace the crown shape to make a paper pattern (fig. 2).
4. Pin the paper pattern to a piece of black felt and cut out. Roll the felt into a cone shape and stitch the edges together to form a crown using either an overcast stitch or a running stitch if you prefer to overlap the edges (fig. 3).
5. Stuff the crown with fiberfill, then stitch the crown to the center of the brim.
6. Sew or glue a band of silver braid around the crown to cover the stitches and another band around the outside edge of the brim.
7. Sew or glue small silver sequins to the brim for decoration.
8. To make a tie for the hat, attach a length of black, lightweight yarn from one side of the hat to the other. Slip a black bead onto the yarn and knot to keep the bead from slipping off (fig. 4). Hang the ornament by this tie.

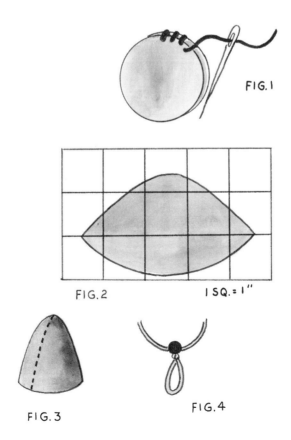

FIG. 1

FIG. 2   1 SQ. = 1"

FIG. 3   FIG. 4

"Tin" Ornaments

The folk artist of Mexico uses inexpensive and easily shaped tin to produce a variety of ornamental Christmas items. The tin is embossed with basic, simple motifs that have been used through the years by artists working in different materials. The tin ornaments are then painted with brilliant transparent turquoise, magenta, yellow, red, and green paints, expressing the Mexican's passionate love of color.

MATERIALS AND TOOLS

Paper for patterns
Pencil
Scissors
Stiff aluminum foil (disposable baking sheets sold in grocery stores or recycled foil from TV dinners or frozen pies are ideal)
Masking tape
Newspapers
Paintbrush—small watercolor brush
Orangewood stick or popsicle stick
Curved manicure scissors
Transparent glass paints or bright, permanent, felt-tip pens
Needle to punch hole for hanging
Nylon fishing line for hanging

HOW TO MAKE

1. Enlarge and trace 1 or more of the suggested ornaments onto paper to make a pattern (fig. 1). Cut out.

2. Create a design on the paper pattern using decorative Mexican motifs. See the examples of motifs shown in fig. 2.

3. Attach the paper pattern to a sheet of aluminum foil with masking tape; then place the foil on a pad of newspapers.

4. Transfer the pattern and all the details to the foil by using the rounded end of a small watercolor paintbrush.

5. Remove the paper pattern and go over the entire design again with the tip of the paintbrush. This is the underside of your work.

6. Now turn the foil over to the front side. Work the tip of the paintbrush just outside the ridges carefully and slowly to push the background down and away from the design. Use an orangewood stick or popsicle stick for working the background that is not close to the ridges.

7. When the entire design has been pushed out, turn to the back side again and work the design out with the orangewood stick.

8. Continue working both back and front to emphasize details and to make the design stand out.

9. After you are finished with the design, use manicure scissors to trim away the excess foil from around the ornament.

10. Paint the ornament with transparent glass paints or with bright, permanent, felt-tip pens.

11. Using a needle, pierce a hole at the top of the ornament.

12. Thread a length of nylon fishing line through the hole and knot ends together.

FIG. 1

1 SQ. = 1"

FIG.2

NETHERLANDS

Hollow Egg Scenes

The Dutch settlers in America decorated their Christmas trees with hollow eggshells filled with miniature scenes. It is also to the Dutch that Americans owe their Santa Claus. When the Dutch came to America in the seventeenth century, they brought with them their tradition of *Sinterklaas*.

MATERIALS AND TOOLS

Egg
Pencil
Transparent tape
Curved manicure scissors
Plaster of paris
Paintbrush
Acrylic paints
Krylon Spray Fixative® (or other permanent protective coating)
White glue—clear-drying
Miniature objects (look in hobby and craft shops and shops that sell doll-house items)
Decorative trim—rickrack, lace, ribbon, braid, or yarn
Long needle
Colored cord or thread for hanging

HOW TO MAKE

1. Without removing the contents of the egg, use a pencil to draw a line where you want to make the oval opening (fig. 1). Place a strip of transparent tape over the penciled line to reinforce the shell before cutting.

2. Cut into the shell with curved manicure scissors, starting well inside the penciled line. Work outward until you can cut along the penciled line without tearing the shell. Do all the cutting while the shell is still moist.

3. Remove tape, rinse inside shell, and let dry.

4. Mix a small amount of plaster of paris, about $\frac{1}{4}$ cup, with enough water to make the plaster the consistency of thin pudding. Paint the inside of the shell with a thin coating of the plaster. Then fill the bottom of the shell with plaster up to the opening. Let dry for a day.

5. Paint the inside of the egg with acrylic paints to create a setting, such as sky, grass, and trees, for the miniature objects. Let dry. The outside of the egg can also be painted with acrylic paints. If you prefer to leave the egg its natural color, spray it with a permanent protective coating to strengthen it.

6. Glue the miniature objects, no larger than $1\frac{1}{4}$ inches high, inside the egg. Let dry.

7. Glue braid, ribbon, rickrack, lace, or yarn around the opening. This will also cover any jagged cutting edges on the egg.

8. To make a loop for hanging, pierce a hole through the shell and plaster *while still wet* with a needle. Run a double strand of colored cord or thread through the hole and knot so that the knot remains inside the shell.

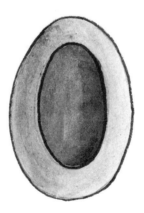

FIG. 1

POLAND

Straw Doll

People living in the Northern, Central, and Eastern countries of Europe make many of their Christmas ornaments from farm materials, such as feathers, blown-out eggshells, and straw.

MATERIALS AND TOOLS

Straw (look in open fields, florist's shops, or feed stores)
Ruler
Scissors
Embroidery thread—red, green, yellow
Wooden bead for head
Paintbrush
Acrylic paints—black, red
White glue—clear-drying
Nylon fishing line for hanging

HOW TO MAKE

1. Peel off the outer coating of the straw and use the shiny inner stalk. Soak the straw in hot water overnight. Keep the straw damp while working so it will remain pliable.

2. To make the dress, cut about 40 straws, each 4 inches long. Line the straws up evenly and tie tightly together with red embroidery thread $\frac{1}{2}$ inch down from the top, to make a neck (fig. 1).

3. To make the sleeves, cut about 10 straws, each 3$\frac{1}{2}$ inches long. Line the straws up evenly and tie tightly together with red or green embroidery thread, $\frac{1}{2}$ inch from each end of the bundle of straws (fig. 2).

4. To make the bodice, place $\frac{1}{2}$ of the straws of the dress over each side of the arms and tie together under the arms with red or green embroidery thread (fig. 3).

5. Using acrylic paints, paint simple facial features on a wooden bead—2 black dots for eyes and a small red oval for a mouth. Let dry, then glue the bead into the top of the straw dress (fig. 4).

6. To make hair, glue 3 straws, each about $\frac{3}{4}$-inch long, into the hole at the top of the bead, letting about $\frac{1}{2}$ inch of the straws stick out beyond the hole. Glue 8 straws, each about 1 inch long, evenly around the top of the bead (fig. 5). Trim if necessary.

7. Cut three 8-inch lengths of yellow embroidery thread. Tie the middle of the 8-inch lengths around the 3 straws sticking up from the center of the wooden bead. Divide the lengths of thread into 3 groups and braid them. Secure the end of the braid by tying a bow with red embroidery thread.

8. Attach a loop of nylon fishing line to the back of the doll for hanging.

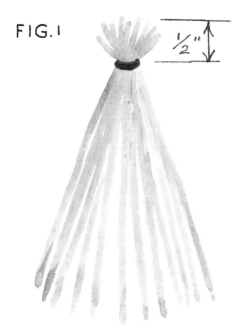

FIG. 1

$\frac{1}{2}$"

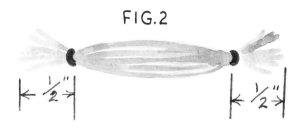

FIG. 2

$\frac{1}{2}$" $\frac{1}{2}$"

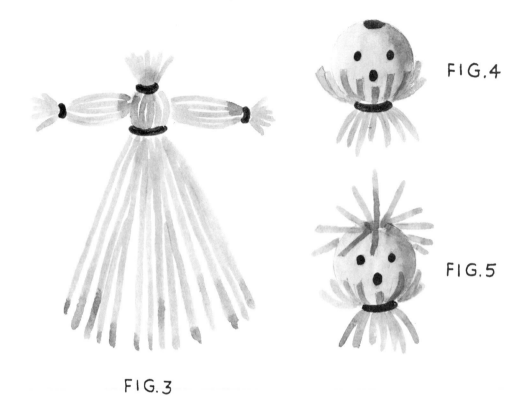

FIG.4

FIG.5

FIG.3

Egg Pitcher

The Polish people make miniature pitchers out of eggshells for Christmas tree decorations. The pitchers are decorated with paper cutouts called *Wycinanki*. The *Wycinanki* craft of paper cutting and pasting first appeared early in the nineteenth century when farming families decorated their homes with beautiful cut paper designs.

MATERIALS AND TOOLS

Egg
Needle
Construction paper
Pencil
Ruler
Scissors
White glue—clear-drying
Lightweight paper—craft, origami, wrapping, or gummed paper
Krylon Spray Fixative® (or other permanent protective coating)

HOW TO MAKE

1. To empty the egg, warm it slightly in a bowl of hot water, then puncture a small hole in each end of the egg with a sharp needle. Be sure to pierce the yolk and membrane. Blow into one of the holes forcing the contents out the other hole. Wash the eggshell, then let the inside dry for several hours or overnight.

2. To make the neck of the pitcher, cut a $1\frac{3}{4}$-inch square from colored construction paper. Fringe one side of the square by cutting $\frac{1}{8} \times \frac{1}{2}$-inch strips (fig. 1).

3. Wrap the neck around the top of the egg, gluing

the 2 ends together and each strip to the egg (fig. 2).

4. Cut a spout for the pitcher from construction paper the same color as the neck. Cut in a diamond shape with a 1-inch length and a 1-inch width (fig. 3). Glue to the neck (fig. 4).

5. Make a handle from a $\frac{1}{2}$ x $3\frac{1}{2}$-inch strip from construction paper the same color as the neck and spout. Using scissors, round the ends of the strip. Glue one end of the handle to the top of the neck and the other end to the egg (fig. 5).

6. Using some of the Polish designs suggested in fig. 6, cut small paper cutouts from colorful light-weight paper such as craft, origami, wrapping, or gummed paper. Glue the designs to the egg, repeating patterns around the egg.

7. Spray the pitcher with a permanent protective coating.

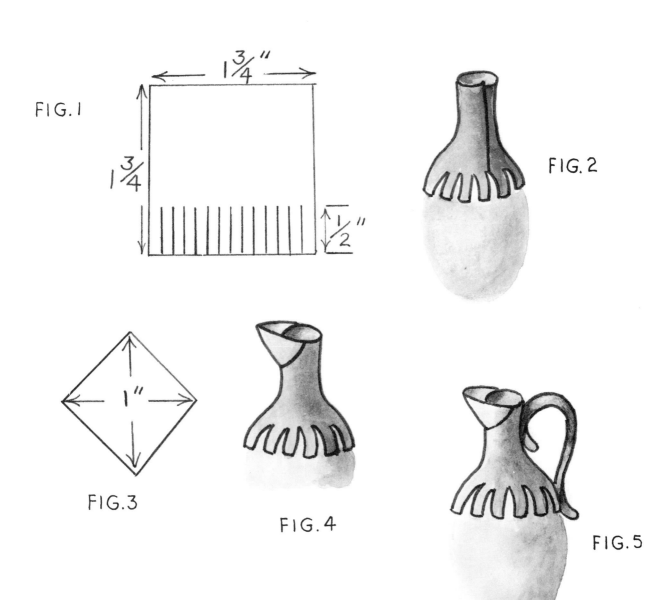

FIG. 1

FIG. 2

FIG. 3

FIG. 4

FIG. 5

FIG. 6

Angel

The Polish people make a unique Christmas ornament—an angel with a heart for her mouth, a crown on her head, and a star in her hand.

MATERIALS AND TOOLS

Paper for pattern
Pencil
Scissors
⅛-inch plywood—4 x 7 inches
Jigsaw or coping saw
Sandpaper
Paintbrush
Gesso
Acrylic paints—assorted colors
Calico fabric scraps
Iron-on interfacing
White glue—clear-drying
Fabric trim—narrow lace, rickrack, or other trim
Nylon fishing line for hanging

HOW TO MAKE

1. Trace the angel pattern onto paper (fig. 1). Cut out and trace around the pattern onto plywood. Use a jigsaw or coping saw to cut out. Smooth the edges with sandpaper.

2. Paint both sides of the angel with gesso to seal. Let dry.

3. Using acrylic paints, paint front and back sides of the angel—an orange crown, yellow star, white wings, yellow, brown, or black hair, flesh-colored face, feet, and hands. Be sure to wait until the face is dry before painting on the facial features. Paint blue eyes, pink cheeks, and a red, heart-shaped mouth (fig. 2).

4. Trace the dress pattern onto paper (fig. 3). Cut out.

5. Iron interfacing to the back of the calico. Trace the dress pattern onto the interfacing, cut out, and glue in place on the wood. Repeat for the other side of the angel.

6. Glue narrow rickrack, lace, or other trim onto the dress.

7. Paint the narrow wooden edge around the dress the same color as the background color of the calico dress.

8. Drill a hole for hanging. See the X on the pattern for placement of hole.

9. Thread a length of nylon fishing line through the hole and tie ends together.

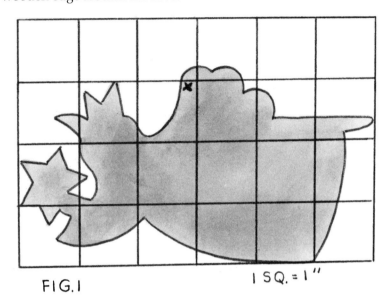

FIG. I   1 SQ. = 1"

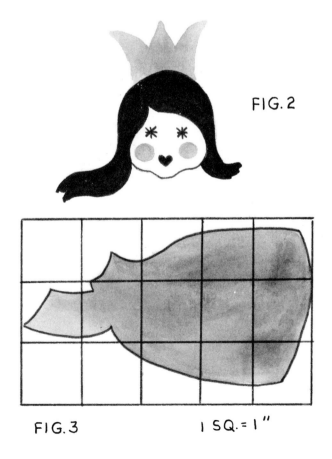

FIG. 2

FIG. 3   1 SQ. = 1"

Porcupine Ball

The people in Poland decorate their Christmas trees with all sorts of bright paper ornaments. The "porcupine ball" originated in Poland and is traditionally used as a tree ornament.

MATERIALS AND TOOLS

Compass
Gift-wrap paper
Scissors
Ruler
Pencil
Quarter
Paper punch
Gummed reinforcement rings (look in stationery shops)
White glue—clear-drying
Needle with large eye
String

HOW TO MAKE

1. Use a compass to make 12 circles, each 4 inches in diameter, on a sheet of colorful gift-wrap paper. Cut out.

2. Using a ruler and pencil, divide each paper circle into 8 equal parts. Draw a small circle in the center of each paper circle by tracing around a quarter (fig. 1).

3. Punch a small hole in the center of each small circle with a paper punch and stick a gummed reinforcement ring around the holes.

4. Cut along the lines leading to the center circle, but do not cut beyond the line made with the quarter. This will give you 8 flaps (fig. 2).

5. Wrap each of the 8 flaps into a cone shape and secure with glue (fig. 3). Repeat this for each of the 12 circles.

6. Thread a needle, with a large eye, with string. Pass the needle through the 12 centers, then gently pull the string until the pointed ends spread into a ball. Tie the thread ends firmly.

7. Attach a loop of string to the ball for hanging.

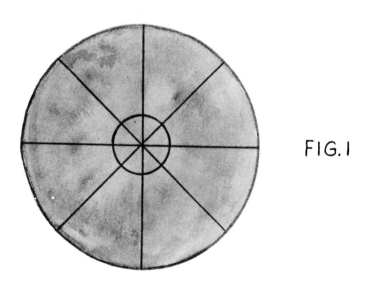

FIG. 1

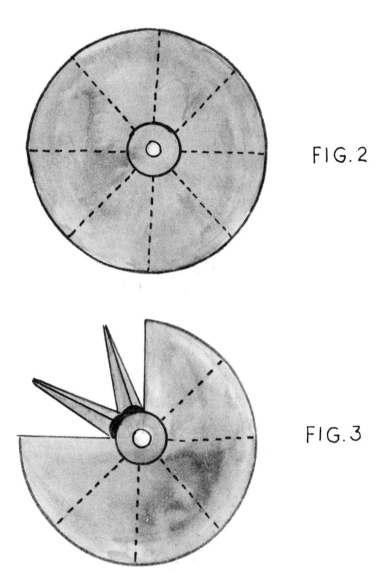

FIG. 2

FIG. 3

RUSSIA (U.S.S.R.)

See: Italy—Befana the Christmas Witch, or, Babouschka the Russian Christmas Witch, page 92.
See also: Ukraine—Spider Web, page 133.

SWEDEN

Straw Garland

In many cultures, wheat symbolizes good fortune. In Sweden, wheat-straw stars and snowflakes are used as tree decorations and are also hung above the holiday table.

MATERIALS AND TOOLS

Straw (look in open fields, florist's shops, or feed stores)

Ruler

Scissors

Button or carpet thread

Red cord or yarn

White glue—clear-drying

Needle

Thread

HOW TO MAKE

1. Peel off the outer coating of the straw and use the shiny inner stalk. Soak the straw in hot water overnight. Keep the straw damp while working so it will remain pliable.

2. Cut about 20 straws, each about $3\frac{1}{2}$ inches long, for each cluster. Tightly tie each cluster in the center with thread so the cluster spreads from the center (fig. 1). The number of clusters you make depends on the length of garland you want.

3. Sew or glue the center of each cluster to a long length of red cord or yarn at 8-inch intervals (fig. 2).

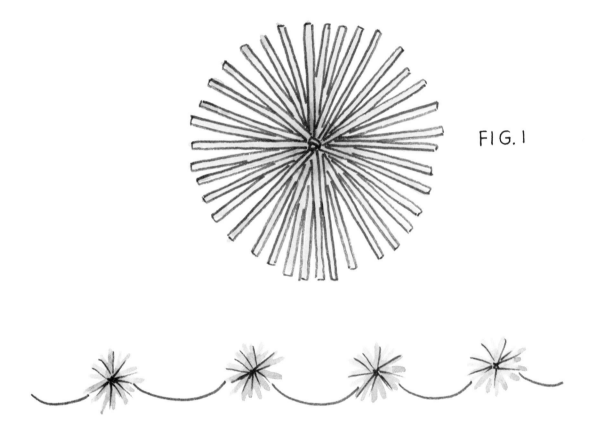

FIG.1

FIG.2

Yule Goat (Julbrock)

The straw goat, in the traditional colors of red, white, and gold, is one of the most popular Christmas decorations in Sweden. Julbrock is meant to be a replica of the goats who pulled Thor (the Norse God of Thunder) in his chariot across the heavens. Like Santa's reindeer, the straw goat provides transportation for the Swedish gnome Jultomten, as he makes his rounds on Christmas Eve to deliver presents. Another of Julbrock's responsibilities is to guard the Christmas tree and to remind the children to be on their best behavior—or he will butt them.

MATERIALS AND TOOLS

Straw (look in open fields, florists's shops, or feed stores)
Ruler
Scissors
Red cord
White glue—clear-drying
Straight pins
Nylon fishing line for hanging

HOW TO MAKE

1. Peel off the outer coating of the straw and use the shiny inner stalk. Soak the straw in hot water overnight. Keep the straw damp while working so it will remain pliable.

2. For each pair of legs, cut about 18 straws, each 6½ inches long. Line the straws up evenly and secure each leg by wrapping tightly with red cord in 4 places (fig. 1). Hold the cord in place with a dab of glue.

3. For the body and head of the goat, cut about 40 straws, each 6½ inches long. Line the straws up evenly; then pull out 4 straws 1 inch from each end of the bundle for the goat's curled horns and tail. Bend the bundle of straws into an S-curve, and wrap with red cord in 3 places to secure the head and neck (fig. 2).

4. Bend the legs into a U-shape, and then tie them tightly to the body with red cord near the neck and tail (fig. 3).

5. Twist 2 straws together to make each horn. Roll toward the back of the neck and hold in place with a straight pin until dry.

6. Bend a few straws down from the chin to shape whiskers.

7. Thread a length of nylon fishing line through some of the straw near the neck and tie to make a loop for hanging.

FIG.1

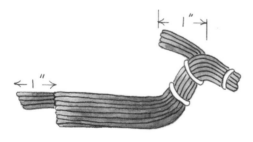

FIG.2

FIG.3

Dala Horse

The toy Dala Horse is from Dalarna (Dalecarlia in English), a province in Sweden. This horse is a decoration used all year round and is a popular souvenir that has come to symbolize Sweden's rustic past. It is traditionally carved from wood, painted red, then decorated with brightly colored designs of hearts, flowers, and greenery.

MATERIALS AND TOOLS

Aluminum foil
Scissors
Ruler
Pencil
Masking tape
Florist's wire—22 gauge to make loop for hanging
Waxed paper
Activa® Products, Inc. Celluclay
Paintbrush
Gesso
Acrylic paints—red, green, gold, blue, white
Krylon Spray Fixative® (or other permanent protective coating)

HOW TO MAKE

1. To make a papier mâché horse, roll a length of aluminum foil into a roll about 4½ inches long. Bend to form a head, neck, and body (fig. 1).

2. Roll a length of aluminum foil into a roll about 5 inches long. Bend in the middle to form the front legs (fig. 2). Repeat to form the back legs.

3. Attach the legs to the body by placing the legs over the body and securing them to the body with masking tape (fig. 3).

4. Insert the twisted ends of a loop of florist's wire into the top of the horse's back to hang the ornament after it is completed.

5. Working on waxed paper, cover and build up the horse with Celluclay. Form ears with Celluclay. Keep your finger moistened with water for easier smoothing. Let dry.

6. Apply a coat of gesso. Let dry.

7. Using acrylic paints, paint the horse red. Let dry. Add painted eyes, mane, tail, harness, and decorative hearts, flowers, and greenery in colors of red, green, gold, blue, and white. See the designs suggested in fig. 4.

8. Spray the horse with a permanent protective coating.

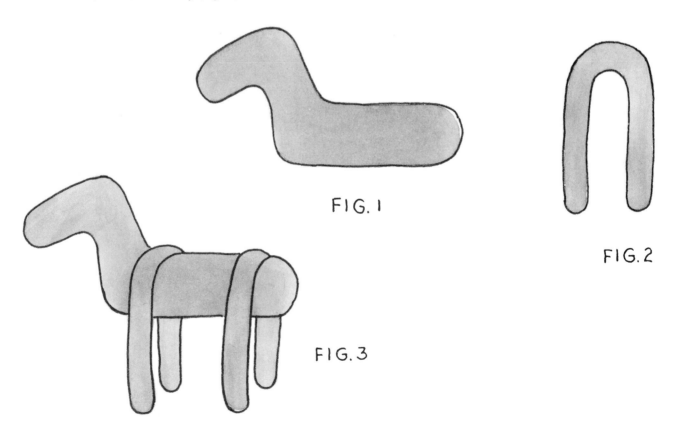

FIG. 1

FIG. 2

FIG. 3

FIG. 4

Heart Basket

The heart-shaped basket, filled with cookies and candies, is a traditional Swedish Christmas decoration symbolizing hospitality.

MATERIALS AND TOOLS

Felt—red, white (each color $2\frac{1}{2}$ x 8 inches)
Scissors
White glue—clear-drying
Ruler
Pencil

HOW TO MAKE

1. Cut out a $2\frac{1}{2}$ x 8-inch piece of red felt and a piece of white felt the same size.

2. Fold each piece of felt in half crosswise; round off at the unfolded ends and cut as shown (fig. 1). In the folded end of each piece, make 4 slits, 2 inches long and $\frac{1}{2}$ inch apart.

3. Hold the red felt cutout in your right hand, the white in your left, with rounded edges facing away from you. Holding them at right angles to each other, weave together as follows:

a. See fig. 2
Insert #1 white strip through inside of #1 red strip; then insert same #1 red strip inside of #2 white strip; insert #3 white strip into inside of same #1 red strip; insert same #1 red strip into inside of #4 white strip; insert #5 white strip into inside of same #1 red strip. Push first completed row to top of slits.

b. See fig. 3
Repeat with second row, this time starting with #2 red strip. Insert the #2 red strip inside the #1 white strip; insert #2 white strip inside of same #2 red strip; insert #2 red strip inside of #3 white strip; insert #4 white strip inside of same #2 red strip; insert same #2 red strip inside of #5 white strip.

c. Repeat for the remaining 3 rows, alternating the color of the starting strip, until entire basket is woven.

4. To make a handle, cut a $\frac{1}{2}$ x $6\frac{1}{2}$-inch felt strip and glue the ends to the insides of the basket.

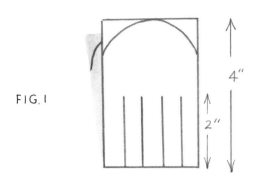

FIG. 1

4"

2"

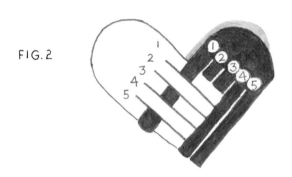

FIG. 2

FIG. 3

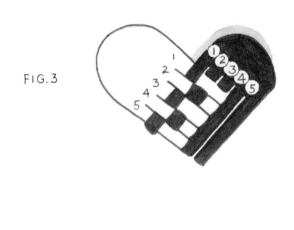

Chip-Cuckoo Bird

According to a Scandinavian legend, many years ago a golden rooster sat on top of a large "world-tree." It was his function to crow at dawn each day to wake up the Norse gods. From this legend came the Swedish Christmas custom of suspending a brightly colored bird or rooster over the dinner table, in a doorway, or from the Christmas tree.

MATERIALS AND TOOLS

Paper for pattern

Pencil

Scissors

$\frac{1}{8}$-inch plywood—6 x 6 inches

Jigsaw or coping saw

Sandpaper

Paintbrush

Gesso

Acrylic paints—yellow, red, black

Drill with $\frac{1}{8}$-inch drill bit

Nylon fishing line for hanging

HOW TO MAKE

1. Enlarge and trace the bird pattern onto paper (fig. 1). Cut out and trace around the pattern onto plywood. Use a jigsaw or coping saw to cut out. Smooth the edges with sandpaper.

2. Apply gesso to both sides of the bird to seal the wood. Let dry.

3. Using acrylic paints, paint the bird yellow, the comb and wattle red, and the eyes red with black centers.

4. Drill a hole at the top of the bird for hanging. See the X on the pattern for placement.

5. Thread a length of nylon fishing line through the hole and knot the ends together.

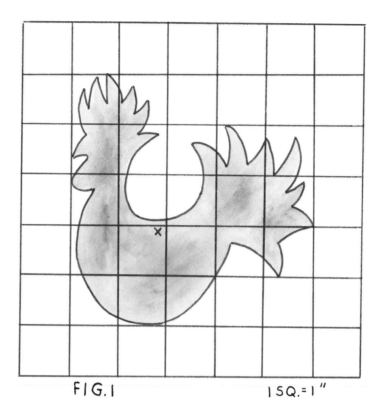

FIG. 1   1 SQ. = 1"

Nut Basket

Basketweaving is one of the most ancient folk crafts, and one found in virtually every culture. The same principles that have always been used in weaving baskets are used today. Baskets are easy and satisfying to make as well as very attractive. Hang this little basket filled with nuts on the Christmas tree.

MATERIALS AND TOOLS

Fine basket reed—(look in craft supply stores)
Ruler
Scissors
White glue—clear-drying

HOW TO MAKE

1. To soften reeds so they won't splinter or break, soak them in water 15 minutes to 1 hour. If the reeds dry out while you're weaving, place your basket in water until the reeds become pliable again.

2. Cross the centers of four 7-inch-long reed spokes. Add a 3⅝-inch reed spoke to the others. This odd spoke will facilitate the over-and-under weaving process. Lash the 5 spokes together, using an 11-foot length of reed called a weaver (fig. 1).

3. After a few wraps around, spread the spokes and begin weaving over and under the spokes with the rest of the weaver until the base is about 1½ inches in diameter (fig. 2).

4. If your weaver should run out before the basket is completed, leave the end behind a spoke and lay a new weaver behind the same spoke (fig. 3).

5. After the base is made, pull the weaver tight and bend the spokes to form a basket shape.

6. To make a border around the top of the basket, cut spoke ends to uniform length, then poke ends down along the spokes (fig. 4).

7. To make a handle, cut three 12-inch lengths of reed and braid together. Insert the braided ends along the spokes inside the basket on opposite sides and glue to secure.

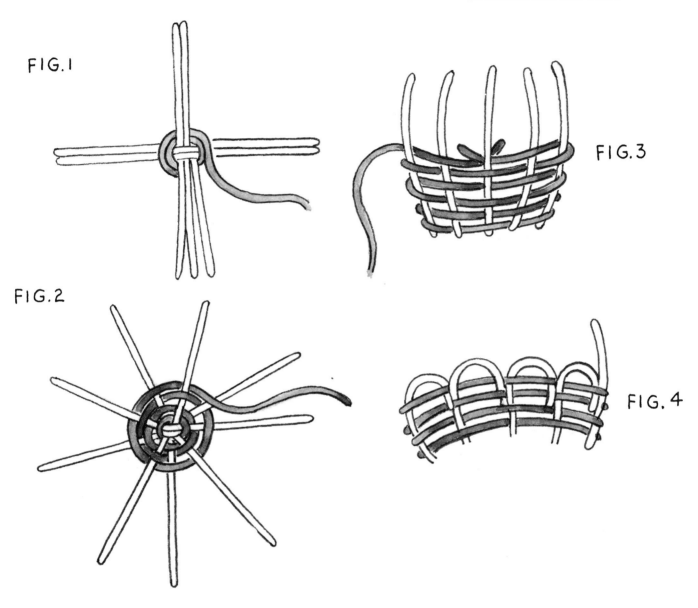

FIG.1

FIG.2

FIG.3

FIG.4

SWITZERLAND

Grattimannen Cookies

In Switzerland on December 6th, Saint Nicholas Day, it is traditional to bake delightful, edible, bread men with raisin eyes and decorative vests and caps of frosted dough.

INGREDIENTS

$2\frac{1}{2}$ cups Bisquick®
$\frac{1}{2}$ cup milk
1 egg
4 tablespoons cooking oil
1 cup flour
Seedless raisins (for eyes)

HOW TO MAKE

1. Mix the ingredients (except raisins) until soft dough forms.

2. Roll the dough thin on a lightly floured surface. Cut with a gingerbread man cookie cutter.

3. Transfer the cookies to a greased cookie sheet. Make hats, vests, boots, suspenders, noses, etc., from separate pieces of dough and assemble the bread men directly on the cookie sheet. Attach these parts firmly and securely to the basic figure. Press raisins into the dough to make eyes (fig. 1). Use a drinking straw to make a hole in the top of each cookie for hanging.

4. Bake approximately 15 minutes or until lightly browned in a 425° F oven.

5. After the cookies cool, decorate with Frosting Paints (recipe below).

6. Thread a length of nylon fishing line through the hole and tie ends together to form a loop for hanging.

FROSTING PAINTS

Beat 3 egg whites until foamy. Add 1-pound box of sifted powdered sugar and the juice from 1 medium-size lemon. Beat until smooth and consistency of heavy cream. Place small amounts into custard cups and tint as desired with liquid food colors. Thin with drops of water to the consistency of paint.

Use a paintbrush to dip into the various frosting colors and paint facial features, vests, buttons, hats, etc.

Yield: About 1 dozen 6-inch-high cookies.

FIG. 1

UKRAINE

Spider Web

In the Ukraine it is considered a sign of good luck to find a spider web in the house at Christmas. This belief originated from a Ukrainian folk tale about a poor woman who had acquired a Christmas tree for her children but was unable to provide trimmings for it. When she awoke Christmas morning, she was overjoyed to find that during the night, the tree had been decorated by a spider who had spun webs over the tree. The morning sunlight falling on the webs turned them to a beautiful silver. Thus, in the Ukraine, imitation webs have been a favorite, traditional Christmas tree ornament throughout the years.

MATERIALS AND TOOLS

Corrugated cardboard—8 x 12 inches
Waxed paper
White glue—clear-drying
Aluminum pie pan or bowl to hold glue
White string
Ruler
Scissors
Straight pins
Paintbrush
Silver glitter
Activa® Products, Inc. Celluclay
Needle
Florist's wire—22 gauge
Acrylic paint—black
Nylon fishing line for hanging (optional)

HOW TO MAKE

1. Prepare a working surface by covering an 8 x 12-inch piece of corrugated cardboard with waxed paper.

2. Pour $\frac{1}{4}$ cup of white glue into an aluminum pie pan or bowl.

3. Cut ten 9-inch lengths and three 30-inch lengths of string. Soak the string in the glue until it becomes thoroughly moistened (about 15 to 20 minutes).

4. Pulling each length of string through the fingers to remove excess glue, place the ten 9-inch lengths into position on the waxed paper as shown (fig. 1). Cut some of these lengths to fit. Gently press the joints together with your finger.

5. Starting from the center of the web, wrap a 30-inch length of string in a spiral fashion over the horizontal, vertical, and diagonal strings. When you come to the end of the 30-inch length, join another 30-inch length and continue the spiral (fig. 2). To help hold the string in place as you wind, push straight pins into the cardboard and wrap the string around them. Remove the pins before the glue dries.

6. After the string web is dry and it is stiff and firm, lightly brush glue over it and sprinkle silver glitter over the glue. Shake off excess glue and let dry.

7. Form a spider shape, about 1 inch long, from Celluclay. Using a needle, make 4 holes on each side of the spider (fig. 3). These will be used later for inserting the wire legs. Let dry.

8. Cut florist's wire into eight 1½-inch lengths; bend to shape legs. Glue, then insert the bent wires into the holes made in the spider (fig. 4).

9. Paint the spider black. Let dry, then glue the spider to the web.

10. Prop up the web on the tree. You can also hang the web if you like, using a length of nylon fishing line.

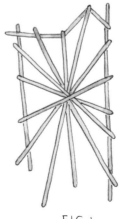
FIG. 1

FIG. 2

FIG. 3

FIG. 4

Pysanky Egg

Pysanky egg decorating is a highly developed, ancient Ukrainian folk art still passed down from generation to generation. The eggs are decorated with many intricate, multi-colored designs drawn on the eggshells using wax and natural dyes. Ukrainian folklore tells us that the fate of the world depends upon the continued tradition of Pysanky egg dyeing. Should the custom cease or be abandoned, a chain holding an evil monster will break and he'll be free to devour us all. The Ukrainian people display these attractive eggs all year round and give them to their friends as a sign of love. Some believe these eggs contain talismanic powers and can protect homes from fire and lightning.

MATERIALS AND TOOLS

Egg
Long needle
Pencil
Felt pens—permanent, fine-tipped in assorted colors
Krylon Spray Fixative® (or other permanent protective coating)
Colored cord or thread for hanging

HOW TO MAKE

Traditional Pysanky egg decorating is a time-consuming, complex method. This adaptation is easier and simpler.

1. To empty the egg, warm it slightly in a bowl of hot water, then puncture a small hole in each end with a sharp needle. Be sure to pierce the yolk and membrane. Blow into one of the holes, forcing the contents out the other hole. Wash the egg shell, then let the inside dry several hours or overnight.

2. Use a pencil to mark off and divide the shell into geometric bands, triangles, and ovals in which further designs can be made. See the designs suggested in fig. 1.

3. Color the designs using brightly colored, per-manent, fine-tipped, felt pens. Usually the designs are repeated symmetrically on the front and back, or top and bottom, of the egg. Let dry.

4. Spray the egg with a clear permanent protective coating. Let dry.

5. To hang the egg, double a length of colored cord or thread through a long needle. Draw the cord or thread through the bottom hole in the egg and up through the top hole. Knot at both ends, leaving a loop at the top of the egg for hanging.

MEANINGS OF DECORATIVE MOTIFS

Stripes, Waves, Ribbons—eternity, everlasting life
Dots—stars, Mary's tears
Eight-Pointed Stars—symbol of Christ
Netting—Christ's fishing for men
Triangle—Trinity
Fish—early symbol of Christianity
Evergreen Tree—eternal youth, health
Wheat—bountiful harvest, good health
Flowers—love, charity, good will
Hens, Storks, Chicks—fertility symbols, wish fulfillment
Deer, Horses—prosperity
Circles—sun, good luck, growth

FIG.1

Other Tree Themes

PARADISE TREE

In the Middle Ages, "mystery plays" were performed in Germany and used by the clergy to teach the important points of Christianity. One of the most popular of the mystery plays was the Paradise play, performed on December 24th. This play dramatized the lives of Adam and Eve. An evergreen tree with apples suspended from its branches was one of the props representing the Garden of Eden. The evergreen tree symbolized immortality and the apples symbolized Adam's fall and were a sign of sin. The play usually ended with the promise of the coming Savior. After the plays were no longer performed, many of the faithful German people set up evergreen trees decked with apples in their homes.

In the fifteenth century, small, round, white wafers were added to the tree, symbolizing the Sacred Host. These wafers were later replaced with cookies in the shapes of angels, flowers, hearts, and bells made from white dough. Later, other cookies were added in the shapes of men, birds, dogs, and other animals made from brown dough. This evergreen tree was the forerunner of our Christmas tree and from the apples came our ornaments of today.

You can trim this novel tree by tying fresh apples to its branches; however, they are not as easy to attach as artificial ones. You can purchase plastic apples or make your own from papier mâché. Also, tie different cookie figures made from the two kinds of dough to the branches. You can keep the tree simple but unusual by limiting your ornaments to the apples and cookies.

Light and Dark Cookies for Paradise Tree

This recipe can be used to make both the light and dark cookies for the Paradise Tree.

DARK COOKIES

INGREDIENTS

4 cups sifted all-purpose flour

4 teaspoons baking powder

½ teaspoon salt

⅓ cup butter or margarine

⅓ cup firmly packed, light brown sugar

⅔ cup light molasses

1 egg

1 teaspoon vanilla

HOW TO MAKE

1. Sift flour, baking powder, and salt onto waxed paper.

2. Beat butter or margarine with brown sugar until fluffy in medium-size bowl. Beat in molasses, egg, and vanilla.

3. Stir in flour mixture, ⅓ at a time, blending well to make a stiff dough. Chill until firm enough to roll.

4. Roll out dough, ¼ at a time, ⅛ inch thick on lightly floured surface. Cut into animal shapes, using cookie cutters or cardboard patterns, cutting out dough around the patterns with a sharp knife. See Patterns for Cookies on page 138. On the Paradise Tree of the past, the

dark dough was used for cookies shaped as birds, lions, roosters, dogs, and other animals.

5. Use a drinking straw to make a hole in the top of each cookie for hanging.

6. Place cookies 1 inch apart on greased cookie sheet. Bake in 350° F oven for 8 minutes or until firm.
Yield: About 4 dozen 4-inch-high cookies

LIGHT COOKIES

Use the same directions and ingredients as for the Dark Cookies, but substitute ⅔ cup honey for the molasses and 1 teaspoon lemon extract for the vanilla. On the Paradise Tree of the past, the light dough was used for cookies shaped as angels, stars, flowers, bells, and hearts.

PATTERNS FOR COOKIES   1 SQ. = 1"

SUGARPLUM TREE

A "Sugarplum Tree" can be made following the early custom of decorating Christmas trees almost entirely with ornaments that could be eaten throughout the holidays or be teasingly tempting until the tree was dismantled after the holidays.

This delicious tree can be decked with a dazzling array of marzipan figures, gingerbread men, pretzel cookies, lollipops, popcorn balls, and candy canes, individually tied to the tree with colorful yarn or ribbon.

Cornucopias, miniature baskets, and other small containers, laden with nuts, cookies, and assorted Christmas candies such as peppermint lozenges, ribbon candy, etc., can also be attached to the tree branches.

Small, colorful candies that are too small to be tied individually to the tree, such as jellybeans, can be displayed by wrapping them in clusters in clear plastic wrap. Place the candies in the center of a square of plastic wrap, then gather the corners and twist tightly. Tie with a pipe cleaner, looping it at the top for hanging. The wrapped candies can then be tied to the tree with a ribbon bow.

Popcorn chains and garlands of candies wrapped in brightly colored paper can be draped around the tree. Staple the papers covering each candy end to end or run a string through the papers so that the candies hang down from the string.

Children as well as adults will be delighted with a Christmas tree decorated with ornaments from Santa's kitchen.

EGG TREE

Trim this tree using just eggs—eggs with scenes inside the shells, eggs with pictures or designs painted or glued to the outside of the shells, egg cups, etc. A variation of this theme is to use only one of these methods, such as the Pysanky method, of decorating eggs for the entire tree.

An attractive way to light the "Egg Tree" and give it a soft, natural glow is to use eggshell lights. Gently tap the rounded end of a large egg with a sharp-pointed object to make a hole large enough to insert a miniature pointed light from a string of miniature lights. Make another tiny hole in the pointed end of the egg. Empty the contents of the egg by blowing through the opening into a bowl. Rinse the inside of the shell and let it dry. Do as many eggs as needed for your string of lights. Insert the miniature lights into the empty shells and tape the wire over the opening with $\frac{1}{4}$-inch adhesive tape applied in crisscross fashion.

SANTA'S WORKSHOP TREE

Miniature sleds, dolls, kites, drums, hobby horses, and other miniature toys can be attached to the tree along with children's play hammers and other tools, small paintbrushes, and jars of paint. Use the leprechaun figures shown in this book for Santa's helpers.

TRADITIONAL TREE

The traditional tree is usually loaded with a miscellaneous assortment of ornaments collected or handed down over the years. Part of the delight of decorating this tree is the recollection with each ornament of special memories of past Christmases. You can make those ornaments in this book that especially appeal to you without concern for any definite tree style to add to your collection of memorabilia. Hang the old and new trimmings side by side on your tree.

ANCESTRAL TREE

Making trims for this tree gives you the opportunity to become acquainted with your own cultural heritage. Trim the tree with ornaments that represent your ancestor's country—or countries—of origin.

FANTASY TREE

Place the Scandinavian elves and gnomes, Irish leprechauns, clothespin fairies, and papier mâché toadstools on the tree and surround them with ropes or clusters of acorns, pine cones, nuts, etc., to give a wooded effect.

DOLL TREE

Use look-alike dolls made primarily from one material such as clothespins, corn husks, or nuts; or use all dolls shown in this book from different countries on the same tree.

PATRIOT'S TREE

Trim the tree with clothespin soldiers, cardboard drums, small American flags, and candles.

STAR OR HEART TREE

Many people collect objects in the shape of a favorite motif, such as a star or heart. Either of these shapes make charming tree ornaments. The heart motif is used in the Swedish heart basket, pincushions, Mexican "tin" heart, and the Czechoslovakian wooden heart. The star motif can be found in the Scandinavian wooden stars and the patchwork stars.

ANIMAL TREE

Many of the animals shown in this book can be used to trim this tree. For example, try the Mexican clay animals, Japanese cat, Swedish goat and horse, Ecuadorian bread-dough turtle, and so forth.

BIRD TREE

A tree can be trimmed with birds made from one kind of material. Or it can be trimmed with an assortment of birds made from different materials. The origami peacocks with their bright, striking colors make a vivid, attractive tree. The natural birds made with pine cones and nuts make a warm, earthy tree.

PATCHWORK TREE

Decorate the entire tree only with patchwork ornaments, such as the stars, trees, and animals shown in this book.

Bibliography

Many of these books are now out-of-print but can be consulted at your local library.

Albaum, Charlet. *Ojos de Dios and Eye of God.* New York: Grosset and Dunlap, 1972.

Ames, Kenneth L. *Beyond Necessity: Art in the Folk Tradition.* New York: Norton, 1978.

Bacon, Lenice Ingram. *American Patchwork Quilts.* New York: William Morrow, 1973.

Bishop, Robert A. *A Gallery of Amish Quilts.* New York: E.P. Dutton, 1976.

Brock, Virginia. *Piñatas.* Nashville, Tennessee: Abingdon Press, 1977.

Christy, Betty, and Doris Tracy. *Quilling: Paper Art for Everyone.* Chicago, Illinois: Henry Regnery Co., 1974.

Comins, Jeremy. *Latin American Crafts.* New York: Lothrop, Lee and Shepard, 1974.

Emmerling, Mary Ellisor. *American Country: A Style and Source Book.* New York: Clarkson N. Potter, 1980.

Espejel, Carlos. *Mexican Folk Crafts.* Barcelona: Editorial Blume, 1978.

Fawdry, Marguerite. *Chinese Childhood.* London: Blaketon Hall Limited, 1977.

Foley, Daniel. *Christmas the World Over.* Philadelphia: Chilton Books, 1963.

————. *The Christmas Tree.* Philadelphia: Chilton, 1960.

Freed, Arnold, et al. *Christmas Holiday Book.* New York: Parents' Magazine Press, 1972.

Gladstone, M.J. *A Carrot for a Nose.* New York: Charles Scribner's Sons, 1974.

Harvey, Marian. *Crafts of Mexico.* New York: Macmillan, 1973.

Hazelton, Nika Standen. *The Cooking of Germany.* New York: Time Inc., 1969.

Hibbs, Ruth S. *Straw Sculpture Techniques and Projects.* New York: Drake, 1974.

Holstein, Jonathan. *The Pieced Quilt.* Boston: Little, Brown, 1973.

Holz, Loretta. *The How-To Book of International Dolls.* New York: Crown, 1980.

Hoople, Cheryl G. *The Heritage Sampler: A Book of Colonial Arts and Crafts.* New York: Dial, 1975.

Horwitz, Elinor Lander. *Mountain People, Mountain Crafts.* Philadelphia: J.B. Lippincott, 1974.

Jones, Iris Sanderson. *Early North American Dollmaking.* San Francisco: 101 Productions, 1976.

Kainen, Ruth Cole. *America's Christmas Heritage.* New York: Funk and Wagnalls, 1969.

Ketchum, William C., Jr. *American Basketry and Wooden Ware.* New York: Macmillan, 1974.

Klamkin, Charles. *Weather Vanes.* New York: Hawthorn Books, 1973.

Lipman, Jean. *American Folk Art.* New York: Pantheon, 1948.

Lord, Priscilla. *The Folk Arts and Crafts of New England.* Radnor, Pennsylvania: Chilton Books, 1965.

Luciow, Johanna. *Eggs Beautiful: How to Make Ukrainian Easter Eggs.* Minneapolis: Ukrainian Gift Shop, 1975.

Munsterberg, Hugo. *The Folk Arts of Japan.* Rutland, Vermont, and Tokyo: Charles E. Tuttle, 1958.

Neal, Avon and Ann Parker. *Ephemeral Folk Figures.* New York: Clarkson N. Potter, 1969.

Nesi, Ruth and Roberta Helmer Stalberg. *China's Crafts.* London: George Allen and Unwin Ltd., 1981.

Nisizawa, Tekiho. *Japanese Folk Toys.* Board of Tourist Industry, Japanese Government Railways, 1939.

Pettit, Florence and Robert Pettit. *Mexican Folk Toys.* New York: Hastings House, 1978.

Robacker, Earl F. *Arts of the Pennsylvania Dutch.* New York: Castle Books, 1965.

———. *Pennsylvania Dutch Stuff.* Philadelphia: University of Pennsylvania Press, 1944.

Sabine, Ellen S. *American Folk Art.* New York: D. Van Nostrand, 1958.

Sanson, William. *A Book of Christmas.* New York: McGraw-Hill, 1968.

Shoemaker, Alfred. *Christmas in Pennsylvania: A Folk Cultural Study.* Kutztown: Pennsylvania Folklore Society, 1959.

Snyder, Philip V. *The Christmas Tree Book.* New York: Viking Press, 1976.

Temko, Florence. *Folk Crafts for World Friendship.* New York: Doubleday, 1976.

Wendorff, Ruth. *How to Make Cornhusk Dolls.* New York: Arco, 1973.

Wernecke, Herbert. *Christmas Customs Around the World.* Philadelphia: Westminster Press, 1959.